OUR LEADERSHIP CALLING

Our Leadership Calling

Rising Above the Illusion of Fear

YISKAH ROSE

• ENP •
A Canadian Publisher

Copyright © 2018 by Yiskah Rose

www.RaiseUpAStandard.com

All rights reserved. This book or any portion thereof may not be reproduced or used in any manner whatsoever without the express written permission of the publisher except for the use of brief quotations in a book review.

This publication contains materials intended to assist readers in pursuing a healthy spiritual lifestyle, and is for educational purposes only. While the publisher and the author have made every attempt to verify that the information provided in this book is correct and up to date, the publisher and author assume no responsibility for any error, inaccuracy, or omission.

Scriptural references are taken largely from the New King James Bible; as well as other versions, with some alternative translation, as deemed appropriate by the author.

First Printing, 2018. Printed in the United States.

ISBN: 978-1-7752888-0-0

17 7 5 2 8 8 8 0 3

Elevate Now Publishing

Grateful Dedication

**For the glorious, infinite *Creator of the Universe*,
The Source from which all goodness, and wisdom flows.**

I am so grateful that You have opened up to me amazing, transformative insights, which I could never have discovered all on my own. I recognize that all of the truths I have come to understand, perfectly belong to You.
In You, I place all my trust.

For my amazing husband Brett.

You have been an unspeakable gift in my life, and have been a tremendous support in my endeavors to write this book. You have encouraged me, inspired me and helped me in so many ways. I am beyond grateful to be with you as we journey together on this adventure of life.

For my three boys: Asher, Jacob and Noah.

It has been an incredible pleasure to welcome each of you into our family. You have all become a gorgeous source of inspiration for me – to face my fears, and to pursue greatness in my life. In turn, I sincerely hope that my life will become a source of inspiration to all of you, as well, as you discover your life calling, and grow into the leaders that you are each uniquely designed to be.

Contents

INTRODUCTION	i
1. Intrinsic Truths	1
2. Fear in the Garden	15
3. Consciousness Connection	25
4. The Serpent Mediator	37
5. The Essence of Leadership	57
6. A Craving for Human Kingship	75
7. Prince With El	101
Notes	133

Introduction

There is beauty in the unknown. Yet, for so long we've been conditioned to run away from it. We've been programmed to believe that we need to *know*, or that we need to *figure things out*, in order to be safe. We have felt the manic need to be in control somehow, in a desperate attempt to escape from our insecurities. Along with this, countless people have been misled into believing that they need to have the "right" recipe of religious doctrine if they are ever going to meet that seemingly impossible goal of "pleasing God."

But, what if this is all a lie?

What if *in the unknown* we will find our greatest potential?

What if *not knowing* is one of the most precious gifts we have?

What if *eating of the tree of our <u>own</u> knowledge* means that we are enslaving ourselves to the limitations of our own conception?

This is not to say that we ought not to treasure truth. Yet, somehow, we need to become okay with the fact that we don't have all the answers, and that we never will. We need to aptly acknowledge that this is not our job.

"Trust… and lean not on your own understanding." (Pro. 3:5)

What we *can* do, however, is connect with the infinite Source of truth. In line with this, we will need to let go of the belief that we can personally heap up the answers in our own mind, and instead allow our minds to venture freely out into the gorgeous abyss of universal wisdom.

If we are to step into the reality of *who we truly are*, we need to begin to see all of the dogma that we have previously swallowed for what it actually is. We need to step back from it all, and realize that allowing ourselves to move into the unknown also means that we are migrating straight into the loving hands of the Divine – where anything is possible, and where everything is ultimately good. We need to connect with a deep trust in the Divine, and truly *know* that we are always safe with Him.

One of the most valuable lessons that I have learned through the course of my life is the value of sincere *openness* in our spirit. Our hearts must become open if we are to become a space for the loving Spirit of the Divine to flow through. If we long for freedom, we will only find it by means of becoming *spaciousness*. With this noble quest in mind, we will need to learn to let go of things, and to no longer identify with that which is false. We need to drop all of the baggage that we heap upon ourselves, and all the weight that we have been carrying for so long. We need to realize that this baggage is not who we are. We need to discover our true identity, which is accompanied by freedom, flexibility, lightness, and opportunity.

The Hebrew Scriptures speak to us of the *heart of stone* that is distanced from the Divine. It is this heavy, burdened, toughened heart that has become the global norm. It is a heart with many hard layers, which is closed to the flow of the Creator. The stone shell of this heart needs to be cracked open. It needs to be chipped away, and eventually completely dissolved. Each layer needs to be peeled off, getting us increasingly closer to full flexibility in our person. Yes, the process of doing so will involve confusion and pain, at times. It will certainly involve facing our fears. Yet the process will yield the most amazing sense of aliveness that makes every passing pain feel like *nothing* in comparison.

Throughout this book, we'll be considering the overall concept of *leadership*. Stepping into authentic leadership that aligns with our Divine calling will mean that we become the original *self* of His design. It means that we stop chasing "self" on the outside, and start realizing who we are, in a deep and lasting sense. Accordingly, as we consider what it truly means to be a leader, we will delve into territory that is unknown for most people.

This unknown territory may very well stir up feelings of discomfort, as we are presented with new ideas. For this reason, we need to be aware that our immediate reactions can lead us astray, because of the fact that many of them are rooted in fear. We also need to be aware that not all of the thoughts that arise from our subconscious are true, since much of our thinking is based upon ideologies that we have been fed in the past. Furthermore, we need to understand that it is also not helpful to be swayed by our automatic feelings, as certain kinds of emotions can easily be triggered by our past conditioning, in tandem with the nervous system's *fight, flight or freeze* response. These are all aspects of our physicality that we will need to master with insightful understanding, as we move forward into higher things.

The journey of discovering our *true self* is an amazing adventure, requiring our personal commitment. On this road, success will become accessible to us when we employ the elements of trust, openness, honesty, humbleness, joy, love, prayer, and meditation, to assist us along the way.

What is more, we are profoundly blessed in that we have an infinitely magnificent Creator, Who wants us to experience success in *all* aspects of life. Let us then approach our life-journey with the willingness to joyously receive everything that the Divine is calling us to receive, and freely open ourselves to finding our unique leadership calling.

"The guidance of Yah lasts forever, the intention of His heart: generation after generation."

(Psalm 33:11)

I

Intrinsic Truths

Each of us has a *leadership calling* on our lives. This is what we were designed for. This is what we have forgotten. This is what we are being reawakened to.

We have forgotten who we really are. The leadership calling on each of us is not the ego-oriented dominance that we have all been accustomed to. Rather, we are called to become leaders in a way that is perfectly harmonious with others, and with our responsibility in relation to the entirety of creation. We are called to become leaders that are neither distracted by our outward status in the world, nor focused on controlling those around us. We are called to become leaders that are full of love and compassion, while being in tune with our authentic-selves in the process. We are called to become leaders that are connected to the Divine, as well as to our own Spiritual essence.

It is beautiful to consider that this is the future of our planet. For those of us who believe in the Divine significance and relevance of the Hebrew Scriptures, we know that the earth will one day be filled with the glory of the eternal, boundless Creator. We further anticipate that the nature of this glory is directly related to the earth being filled with people who have finally realized who they really are: family to the Divine, connected to infinite potential, and greatly loved.

Each of us has a distinctly unique blueprint – a part of the gorgeous mosaic of Divine manifestation. We are all connected, yet each of us is an individual facet in the ultimate diamond of a bona fide human collective. Because of this uniqueness, we cannot find our true self from the outside. No one else can show us who we are, and what we are here to do. We are not born to "*fit in*." We are born to "*stand out*" and to be a witness to the invisible reality of our Divine calling and the special talents that dwell within us. This is the gift of our being.

It is only by learning to love ourselves, and by connecting to the Creator, that we will finally be freed to become "me." Our true *me* is also deeply connected to the true *me* of others. In this way, when we find ourselves, we also find the true community and connection that we have always longed for. And, by learning to connect with our self, we give others the space to be themselves as well. We will receive the beauty and love of other unique and connected people. We will rejoice in the expressed wisdom, talents, and contributions of others, without feeling outshined or even threatened by their accomplishments.

This description of harmonious being is a beautiful picture of what is possible. What is even more beautiful is the fact that it *will be*. It's a Divinely promised future for all of true humanity. It's a future that we can even begin to step into today, and then in increasing degrees, throughout the course of our lives. We only need to courageously choose it: to choose the road that leads into the astounding depths of Divine truth and unthinkable reality.

This is the road that I have chosen. It is a glorious road, wherein I rejoice to *stand, walk, run, leap* and *fly* alongside of others who have also chosen to leave the path of the false external world: to jump in with both feet and discover the joy of that which is far beyond anything that is now understood to be in the realm of possibility.

"Those who wait on YHWH shall renew their strength; they shall mount up with wings like eagles, they shall run and not be weary, they shall walk and not faint." (Isa. 40:31)

Blueprint for Healing

It is gorgeously astounding to consider that we have been spoken to by the One Who is completely beyond comprehension for us – the One Who is eternal and infinite – the One Who even the heaven of heavens cannot contain. That select expressions, ideas and intentions of the Everlasting Creator have been recorded for us is inexpressibly amazing.

The beginning of this Divine Revelation begins with what is known as "*the Torah.*" Therein we find amazing Divine insights that lay the foundation for the rest of the Biblical record.

The Torah is essentially a message for healing, with great significance for all of humanity. It was recorded by Moses, the humble leader who is known for speaking with the Creator "*face to face.*"[1]

The Hebrew word "*Torah*" refers to the first five books of the Bible, and carries the meaning of "*instruction*" or "*teaching.*" It is important to understand that *education* has always been the ultimate purpose of *everything* that we find within the words of these five books. They have been written to teach us, both by action and by meditation on the deep, Spiritual meaning for humanity. The Torah has always been intended to bring us to a place of wisdom, and to provide us with understanding concerning who we *really are*, as opposed to who we have been *taught to be* in the context of our imbalanced, and often unhealthy world.

The purpose of the Torah – its stories, its Mosaic observances, its prescription for Tabernacle worship, its commandments, its statutes – has always been to stretch our mind, transform us, and to bring us to a place of elevated being. In this way, we will be reconnected with our true self, which is the "*me*" that is aligned with the exalted Consciousness of our God. This is really what it means to be His people, His family, His children, and His loved ones.

The interesting nature of the Torah is that it is a mosaic of varying elements and parts: the record of the beginning of creation, historical accounts, stories of individuals, and the significant narrative of the heritage of Abraham and his family. Furthermore, it incorporates various statutes, commandments, instructions, explanations, descriptions of dreams, glimpses into the Divine, personal lessons and, ultimately, an intimate education about our mysterious design.

Even with all of the variable details, as a holistic whole, every detail has depth and purpose. In this sense, everything in the Torah has amazing potential to bring restoration, healing and reconnection from all that we have lost. As I understand it, the nature of this ancient writing is Divine, and in this sense it is infinite, eternal, boundless, and timeless. And, because it is rooted in this Divine origin, it can only be interpreted with the help of the Creator Himself. Unless we determinedly pursue the Creator as we seek to study His writings, we study in vain. We need *His help*, and *His hand* to tune into the Divine. We need to seek Him in all these things.

"For YHWH gives wisdom;
From His mouth come knowledge and understanding;
He stores up sound wisdom for the upright;
He is a shield to those who walk uprightly."
(Pro. 2:6-7)

"For as the rain comes down, and the snow from heaven,
And do not return there,
But water the earth,
And make it bring forth and bud,
That it may give seed to the sower
And bread to the eater,
So shall My word be that goes forth from My mouth;
It shall not return to Me void,

> *But it shall accomplish what I please,*
> *And it shall prosper in the thing for which I sent it."*
> (Isa. 55:10-11)

Undoubtedly, when approaching the early events recorded in the book of Genesis, this common question tends to come up: Are the events "*literal*" or "*allegorical*?" This is not the question that I asked in these studies. My questioning has simply been centered around the following questions: "*Yah, what do You want Your people to know? What does all of this really mean? What is really being communicated to us from You, from Your perspective and outside all of the doctrines, religious lenses, and debates of mankind?*"

Personally, I was brought up to approach all of the details in Genesis in a rigidly literal manner. Yet now, when I have nothing to lose by being open in my approach to these things, I am increasingly finding that the details in early Genesis seem to be more figurative, symbolical and allegorical in nature. Yet at the same time, I believe that they *perfectly represent* what took place in our beginnings in a manner that is true. I have found in the record a narrative that strikingly represents *ultimate and intrinsic truths* that are relevant, applicable, and vitally important to all generations.

In relation to the discoveries that I have found in the details recorded in early Genesis, with their extreme relevance, stunning beauty, amazing value, and far reaching "realness," I no longer feel that I need to struggle with the exactitudes of how literally they present the particulars of what happened at that time in the earth's history. The awareness of how intrinsically true they are, even until today, is so awe-inspiring and worthy of praise, that it leaves me with no worries about what we *don't* know. It is a beautiful reminder that God has given us everything in terms of what we do need, and has not cluttered our lives with things we don't. Truly, we need to learn to ask the right questions, and we need to know the right source to direct our questions *to*. Too much questioning and wrestling has been directed towards each other, or human authorities – yet it is only God Who has the answers – and I feel that I can honestly attest to the fact that He is so willing to give us the answers if sought sincerely (even if it can take us time to open ourselves to them).

Yes, of course we can be of help to one another, learn from each other, and step into the roles of leadership that we are each called to. On the other hand, we must be primarily looking to *The Source* of all truth, wisdom, knowledge and understanding, if indeed those are what we are looking for.

And so, *"What is it that God wants us to know?"* Certainly, there is not one single thing that I can claim He wants us to know. That would be absurd since, after all, He is a Divine and Infinite Being and will continue to reveal whatever He wants to, whenever He wants to. Yet, through the pages of this book I will endeavour to share some truths that I've tapped into, through personally asking this question. Much of these truths are associated with our beginnings, as is found in the first few chapters of *Genesis*.

So back to the question: "What does God want us to know?"

According to what I have come to understand, He wants us to know why He made us. He wants us to know that we were made to be like Him, in His beautiful, glorious image and likeness. In accordance with this, He wants us to know that we are a part of His family, by design, so that we have both great potential as well as great responsibility. The world has become the dark, disastrous place that it is today directly because we have become disconnected from these very things. Yet at the same time, we have been given the amazing ability to bring forth *all good* on this planet – to be a part of its perfectly harmonious design, while we nourish the earth around us. We have been designed to healthfully give and take from the planet in a balanced manner, and also to reap the benefits of our own efforts, as we care for the ground on which we live.

We have been given such awe-inspiring potential to do the impossible, and to hold hands with the Eternal One Who is so willing to show us all the hidden things of His creation. In this way, He is very much a loving Father to us. Yet, in general, much of humanity has manifested as an evil and monstrous machine – bent on destroying all the beautiful things that God has made – and leaving in its place all of the ugliness that comes from the extractive nature of greed. Maybe, as an individual, we think that we are too small to do anything about it. Maybe we feel that we aren't the *real* ones to be held accountable, since we find ourselves outside of the realm of power and leadership in the earth.

But what if this is just a lie we tell ourselves? What if each one of us is called to leadership on the earth? What if our God will hold us accountable for the *supportive role* that we are playing in this evil machine?

I am going to suggest that if we believe that we can't do anything about the current state of affairs in this world, then we are actually believing a lie. And this belief can never really please the One Who has made us for something better. He knows the truth. He knows that we were born to lead – every one of us – by the very fact that we are human beings. He remembers that He put the capacity in us to lead, and He also fully expects us to step into the responsibility that comes with this capacity.

For millennia, humans have been erroneously seeking another human being to be their primary leader. In this, they have forgotten who they really are as men and women. The fact is, we were not originally called to *rule* each other, according to the blueprint of the Creator. We were initially created to the *mutual* responsibility over the creation, to rule *together* over it, with fullness of love, care, and appreciation. Yes, we can be inspirational leaders to each other in various ways, and God has called people to special roles of leadership. That's the very topic of this book. But He has always intended that we rule together, *with Him*, as extensions of His love, in the universe that He has made. The amazing blessing in our day is that we're finally waking up to this fact.

People are waking up to the knowledge that we *do* hold the power to change things for the good, and the right. Today, we can see for ourselves that individuals are beginning to stand up to the evil systems that are still holding the helm in our worldwide human civilization. Instead of "*looking for a king*" to fight our battles for us, people are stepping up to the plate and realizing our own personal responsibility, as well as our potential, to be a part of changing the world with the help and guidance of the Creator.[2]

In my observance, most of the "*changemakers*" in our world today do believe in a "Higher Power" of some kind. Not all of them specifically see the God of Israel as the One True God, but for those of us who do, we need not be concerned about the reality of varying perspectives concerning the Divine in our day. He is the God who has created all of us, and will reveal Himself as He sees fit; as indeed He has been doing now for millennia.

> *"Whatever YHWH pleases, He does, in heaven and in earth, in the seas and in all deeps."* (Psa. 135:6)

> *"O YHWH, the God of our fathers, are You not God in the heavens? And are You not ruler over all the kingdoms of the nations? Power and might are in Your hand so that no one can stand against You."* (1 Chr.20:6)

> *"For YHWH Most High is to be feared, a great King over all the earth."* (Psa. 47:2)

The religions of men have never contained Him, and they never will. Not one of them.

The Divine is Boundless

On a more intimate note, I recently I had a dream in relation to the *out-of-the-box* nature of God. I found this dream to be beautifully insightful for me in my life and in my understanding of Him. (As an aside, I realize I can neither claim to understand everything about dreams, nor where *our* consciousness ends and *His* begins. Yet, many times I have experienced the blessing of my dreams assisting me in my awareness and opening up my understanding.)

In this simple yet vivid dream, I saw all sorts of peoples around the world; all types of religions and denominations, both Biblically-based and otherwise. At the same time in this dream I came to see an Essence of the Presence of God. I saw that this Divine Presence moved all *around* the boxes that these religions were found in. This Presence was never quite entering any of them yet was secretly interacting, in some way, with those who found themselves within the confines of these box-like communities. Furthermore, this Presence was in the dark recesses *between* all of these things, in the hidden black space of darkness.

> *"He made **darkness His secret place**; His canopy around Him was **dark waters** and **thick clouds** of the skies."*
> (Psa. 18:11)

This dream spoke to me of the reality that God's Presence really is everywhere, and that He is willing to work with all of humanity. Surely this is the reason why so many people have experienced Him, to varying degrees, from a multiplicity of religious backgrounds. This dream also speaks to the reality that since His true Presence is *outside* of the man-made religious boxes found in our world, then we cannot find Him in fullness unless we also step outside of these confines, in whatever way He calls us to, in our individual lives. Additionally, this dream seemed to underscore the fact that He loves all of humanity and is willing to work with every single one of us, no matter where we have come from, or what our current belief set happens to be. He will work wherever there is potential for good, and wherever people are seeking His hand. These truths are certainly paralleled in the Hebrew Scriptures as well.

> **"YHWH is high above all nations**, His glory above the heavens." (Psa. 113:4)

> **"All the kings of the earth shall praise You, O YHWH, when they hear the Words of Your mouth.** For great is the glory of YHWH. Though YHWH is on high, yet He regards the lowly..." (Psa. 138:4-6)

The Hebrew Scriptures also promise that the future ahead of us will be different than the world is now. We will all one day awake to the fact that rigid sectarian constructs of man have never served us, but rather have confined and restricted us instead. To a huge extent, they have hidden the true Creator from us, and have disguised our true essence. The promised future is one in which humanity will ultimately put aside all false, limiting beliefs, and turn to find that which is invisible, infinite, boundless and eternal. In unprecedented fashion, we will finally open our hearts to Him. In beautiful tandem with this, then, we will be able to fully receive *each other* into these open hearts as well.

To be sure, it is a strange existence that we now have. So often we don't even see what's right in front of our eyes. We believe what we are told by other people, rather than simply seeing things as they really are. We need to tune back into our own discerning intuition, rather than becoming sponges for the world's false, futile, and destructive ideas.

I am convinced that the Creator of the Universe is calling us to realize our responsibility and our potential. He wants us to perform the responsibility that He has placed in us from the beginning. He intends for us to operate with the breathtaking potential that He has gifted us with: to be like Him, to be His family, to be His people, and to be intimately connected with Him in a loving and cooperative relationship.

If some of the points that I have been sharing seem foreign to you as the reader, that's okay. The summary I have presented thus far will be expanded upon in further chapters, with these ideas being substantiated with additional Biblical details. Each of us has subconscious programming that we will need to face as we move into further truth, and this programming is virtually always rooted in fear – the fears that we have been taught to believe, as well as the fears that are rooted in an absence of truth. So as we continue, may each of us move beyond our automatic programmed reactions with humble hearts that are open to His truth. Whatever His truth may be.

2

Fear in the Garden

After having looked at the distinction between the confining quality of dogmatic, *so-called truth* and the expansive nature of *truth itself*, let's now enthusiastically revisit the Genesis story, anew.   More specifically, let's turn our attention to the entry of humanity into the present reality of the world as we know it today (that is, the reality that has evolved outside of the garden). To do this, we need to turn our attention to Genesis chapter three.

Here we have the account of what is commonly termed "*the temptation and fall*" of humanity, as follows:

Genesis 3:1-7

"Now the serpent was more cunning than any beast of the field which YHWH God had made. And he said to the woman, 'Has God indeed said, you shall not eat of every tree of the garden?'

And the woman said to the serpent, 'We may eat the fruit of the trees of the garden; but of the fruit of the tree which is in the midst of the garden, God has said, you shall not eat it, nor shall you touch it, lest you die.'

Then the serpent said to the woman, 'You will not surely die. For God knows that in the day you eat of it your eyes will be opened, and you will be like God, knowing good and evil.'

So when the woman saw that the tree was good for food, that it was pleasant to the eyes, and a tree desirable to make one wise, she took of its fruit and ate. She also gave to her husband with her, and he ate. Then the eyes of both of them were opened, and they knew that they were naked; and they sewed fig leaves together and made themselves coverings."

There is an amazing depth of hidden truth in this passage for us to consider and meditate upon, but let's zero in on a few details that are specifically relevant to our present discussion.

First of all, I would like to draw your attention to something at the beginning of Genesis which has, for a long time, been a subject of deep meditation for me. It is a thematic detail that most people gloss over, or dismiss, simply because it does not fit in with traditional views associated with this narrative. Yet, it is a detail that has been Divinely and purposefully included, so, consequently, it is well worth seeking to understand.

In Genesis chapter two, it specifically details the command that was given to Adam:

"And YHWH God commanded the man, saying, 'Of every tree of the garden you may freely eat; but of the tree of the knowledge of good and evil you shall not eat, for in the day that you eat of it you shall surely die.'" (Gen. 2:16-17)

Here the Creator commands the man *not to eat* of the *Tree of the Knowledge of Good and Evil*. Yet, when the serpent asks the woman about this commandment, we find that the details she references are noticeably *different* than the command that was initially given by God. In fact, the commandment that Eve quotes includes a very obvious addition to it. We read on to find her false claims that it had been *"God who said"* – not only were they to refrain from *eating* of the forbidden tree's fruit – they were also to completely avoid *touching* it, lest they die.

Later in the Hebrew Scriptures we find a pertinent, repeated principle being expressed in the context of the Creator's instructions. We arrive at the following words that emphasize the value of *only* attributing to God that which is *truly* Divine in origin, and living our lives accordingly:

*"So you shall observe to do **just as YHWH your God has instructed you**; you shall **not turn aside to the right or to the left**."* (Deu. 5:32)

It is curious to consider how Adam and Eve (or at the very least, Eve) had personally devised an addition to the commandment. Nonetheless, there are some well-meaning Bible teachers who have looked at this and concluded that it was a *good idea* for Adam and Eve to have made this addition to God's teaching. Yet, *was* it really a good idea? The later instructions of God to His people would indicate otherwise. As indicated, we are not to turn to the right or left: away from the centered path that God has laid out for us. Or, in other words, we are neither to add nor take away from His perfectly balanced instructions to us.

*"You **shall not add to the word** which I am commanding you, **nor take away from it, that you may keep** the commandments of YHWH your God which I command you."* (Deut. 4:2)

It is essential for us to understand that, although it may *appear* that the additive to God's commandment was a reasonable safeguard against supposedly "breaking" the commandment, the actual reality is that it bred the distorted mindset of fear. It bred fear, not of God, but of the Tree of the Knowledge of Good and Evil. In this way, it exalted and gave power to *the tree*, rather than to God.

And so it is with all human reasoning that supersedes the instructions of our Creator.

Paradoxically, the tremulous headspace that Adam and Eve had created for themselves was the catalyst for their eventual sin. Their unchecked fear skewed their perspective, and made them vulnerable to falling. They allowed it to overwhelm them, and it gave rise to the fateful decision to eat from the forbidden tree.

Their additional command strikingly became the *very reason* for why they ended up eating of the *Tree of the Knowledge of*

Good and Evil. It is beyond ironic that the very thing they intended to safeguard them from breaking the commandment of the Creator, became the critical factor that tore all safety away.

By *adding to* the instruction of Yah, they also ended up *taking away from it*. By means of the serpent's influence they eventually reasoned that it was a good idea to disregard the original, unadulterated Divine edict. Essentially, by adding to it, they also made it *null and void*; and, by their own reasoning, God's pure and simple command finally seemed irrelevant to their existence. It was according to this decidedly imbalanced perception of things where, in *turning to the right hand*, they also found themselves violently swinging to the *left* (symbolically speaking).

The false reality that Adam and Eve induced into being by adding the additional commandment *to not touch the tree* was, in effect, a reality of fear. And since fear only serves to compound upon itself when left unchecked, it ends up creating a life experience that becomes increasingly unbearable. In the case of Adam and Eve in the garden, their personal relationship with their natural environment would have been drastically altered because of the intensifying fear that they allowed into their life. The intensity of their fear of touching the tree, *lest they should die*, would have created the situation in which they would no longer have joyously felt freedom-of-movement within their perfect garden home.

Furthermore, since we can easily come into contact with things accidentally, the false belief that it was forbidden to even *touch* the *Tree of Knowledge of Good and Evil* would quickly lead to the perception that one must also completely steer clear of it. There is always a chance that one should unintentionally, even minutely, brush up against its branches. The question then becomes, *how far away must you stay?* Accordingly, this unfamiliar and uncomfortable territory easily evolves into an even larger fear, wherein the fearful person will begin to avoid the area altogether. In this way, one's focus is no longer directed towards God. Rather, it becomes distorted by fear, and is obsessively directed towards the "*deadly*" tree instead.

On the other hand, if you were not at all concerned about touching the tree, and simply sought to avoid *eating of it* (as God actually instructed in the first place), this means you have the satisfying space to touch it, handle it, observe it, climb it, study it, etc. In other words, you can confidently still be the master of it – without being disturbed by fear. Essentially, this is the principle: just *choose* not to eat it by staying centered in the peaceful, trusting simplicity of aligning with Divine Consciousness and His design.

Moving on, a primary result of the humanly-conceived addition to God's simple law was that they (or at least Eve) became trapped in their fearful, imbalanced state. For that matter, this self-induced fear also made Eve forget who she really was. Hence, by the time the serpent approached Eve to begin discussing this tree, she had critically forgotten that she was *already* made in the image and likeness of God. She forgot that she had a Heavenly Father Who was so ready to give her wisdom, at any time, if she just sought it from Him (see Pro. 3:6). Alternatively, she began seeking wisdom and clarity from another source. Curiously, she unfavorably sought for these elements from the *very tree* that she feared, namely, *the Tree of the Knowledge of Good and Evil*.

The fundamental reason she would have been tempted to pursue Divine *likeness and wisdom* from this outward source, was that she had become disconnected from who she was designed to be, from the very beginning. She had forgotten her true-self. Since the day of her creation, she was already given *likeness to God*, and she already had access to *wisdom* through her relationship with the Creator. Yet, through the act of incorporating false ideologies onto an unchanging law, she became disoriented and confused in her fear. Finally, when presented with the promise that *wisdom would be hers* if she ate from the forbidden tree, she gave in, thus precipitating the disastrous consequences that would follow in her own life, as well as in subsequent generations.

Ever since, peoples of all backgrounds have found it very easy to justify adding to God's laws; even considering it a *high and lofty*, or *Godly* thing to do. Many religious people would mistakenly assume that it is surely not evil to try to *go beyond* the instruction. Nonetheless, the story in Genesis tells us otherwise. Adding to the true standard is delusion, and will ultimately lead to the outright disregard for truth altogether. This is actually of the utmost importance for us as humans to understand, as it is a human blunder that has been repeated countless times throughout history ever since.

For the sake of clarification, it is valuable to consider the concept of wisdom in relation to our present discussion. What is the relationship between wisdom and adhering to specific laws? Wisdom is something that is *additional* to the law, in a sense, but not in the same way as *adding* to the law.

The direct Instructions of the Creator (including universal laws) are unchangeable, and are essentially "fixed," for lack of a better term. At the same time, these dependable, universal laws leave so much room for us to move, and to pursue our amazing potential according to the intention of the Creator. On the other hand, wisdom *itself* is a flexible and moveable quality that takes into consideration the laws of the universe. Decisions based upon wisdom take into account many factors, in order to make a holistic and healthful decision, all in the context of our relationship with God. Wise decision-making also directly involves the Creator, Who will bring insights into our life path when we invite Him to do so.

The Scriptures repeatedly indicate that wisdom comes from a commitment to walking in the Ways of the Creator. On the other hand, *wisdom* and *law* are two distinct, yet interrelated things. We can infinitely build our wisdom upon the laws of the universe, but the moment we seek to solidify and crystalize certain elements of our own wisdom, we have then *"added to the law"* and, in this sense, pulled away from the Design of our God.

In the case of Adam and Eve, while they may have reasoned it to be *wise* to refrain from spending lots of time touching the *Tree of the Knowledge of Good and Evil*, they were obliged to allow their personal perspective regarding wise action to be flexible, and subject to change, along with any further insights they may develop. Unfortunately, though, this was not the case. They made their own *"wise idea"* into the very commandment itself. And so, when Eve was asked about the law of the Creator, she quoted *the amended / added commandment*, rather than the pure instruction that they received from the mouth of their Loving, Eternal Father.

Thus we see that humanly-conceived *fear in the garden* became a primary factor in producing the crystallization of human reason into definitive law. Thereby, an era of bondage and pain was birthed into the world. In this we discover the treacherous malignancy of fear. The hidden fears among people have the potential to become a catalyst for all kinds of insane actions; and when we look back upon the history of humanity upon the earth, we can see fear giving rise to the most unimaginable atrocities done at the hands of men.

Our fears, therefore, *must* be mastered – in every single one of our lives. We must courageously face our fears, feel the discomfort of our fears, and then overcome them by giving them no more power over our lives. This is the dynamic path to freedom, and the prevailing road that we are being directed to pursue – as we open ourselves up to Spiritual revelation, and learn to connect with the elevated Consciousness of the Divine.

3

Consciousness Connection

For millennia, people have been engaged in the practice of attempting to find *outside-of-themselves* that which they already have *within*. While this may seem absurd, it's precisely what we have been programmed to do.

This tendency began at the very beginning in the Garden of Eden as a precursor to *the fall* of Adam and Eve. Having already begun to disconnect from both God and *self*, Eve saw in the *Tree of the Knowledge of Good and Evil* something which gave an impression, or an appearance, of the missing self. Additionally, through her newly affected observance of this tree, she inevitably began to envisage the connection that she had lost through fear. By distorted imagination, the external tree transmuted into something to be embraced as the outward mechanism for gaining wisdom and, ultimately, becoming like God. The grand irony of this is that, in reality, these things were already available to her; they were to be found *within*. She had them all along, but was no longer aware of them. This is simply because fear actively obscures our awareness, and vigorously fogs our perception. It blinds us to what is obviously right in front of us, and in our midst.

As we've already indicated, this practice of pursuing God and self, in an external sense, is a symptom of *fear-based insanity*. People have forgotten what is real, and who they are. This loss of "me" has left a painful void in all of us. Yet, the innate and underlying desire to reconnect with the true *self* has been bulldozed by the societal tendency to fill the void with the outside noise that merely mimics reality, and creates a counterfeit, false self-identity.

As has already been well-discussed by many, the false, external self is typically referred to as the *"ego."* The tendency to seek fulfillment in egoic, external things began at the very beginning, with Eve and the story of partaking of the forbidden tree. Having already begun to disconnect from God and the primordial self, because of fear, Eve began to cling to contrived, artificial promises of connection through the tree. Yet, the best this tree could ever do was imitate true connection – just like any other addiction.

> *"Let us make a name for ourselves… an external tower reaching to the heavens."* (From Gen. 11 – paraphrased)

Hence, the external, visible *"knowledge tree"* began to be falsely perceived as a promise of wisdom, and of likeness to the Creator – both of which were already part of Adam and Eve inwardly, according to the authentic blueprint of the holistic human being. This inward *Spiritual-self* was originally created by God to be the center of who we are as human beings.

It is commonly understood that the *tabernacle* or *temple* is a symbol of the Spiritually-centered human being. In this beautiful representation, the Spirit Presence of the Creator abides in the *Most Holy Place,* which is representative of our innermost being. Appropriately, this gorgeous reality is woven throughout the fabric of the Hebrew Scriptures. In early Genesis, this illustrated truth is originally represented by the *Garden of Eden*. Like the tabernacle, *the garden* is the holistic design of the Spiritual human being. The midst of the garden is the innermost being; there the *Tree of Life* is positioned, and the Presence of the Creator dwells. Here is the place where we can enjoy the unspeakable blessing of connecting to Divine Consciousness.

Interestingly, Genesis chapter two reveals to us that at the center of the inward Spiritual garden, there is a dual positioning of *two* trees: the *Tree of the Knowledge of Good and Evil,* and the *Tree of Life*. What this means, in essence, is that by God's loving design we were given the gift of free will to choose which of the two we would align ourselves with. In this space of profound love and grace, we were given complete freedom of choice. As such, we could choose to put our trust in Him or not. These details are the crux of everything that happens in the early chapters of Genesis.

After this manner, Adam and Eve were given liberty to either choose trust and connection with God, or to distance themselves entirely. For some mysterious reason that we are not told of, however, they did end up distancing themselves from God, producing the situation wherein they began to dwell in distorted fear. They entered into the state of fear, which only has apparent power outside of our *trust* in the One Who made us. And...

- If we don't ***trust*** that our God loves us, we will make evil choices.
- If we don't ***trust*** that God will 'meet with us' to ensure our success and prevent our failure, we will make evil choices.
- If we don't ***trust*** that God's commandments need no amendment, we will make evil choices.
- If we don't ***trust*** that God is Who He is – full of love, care, forgiveness, patience, understanding, mercy and longsuffering – we will make evil choices.

Every one of these evil choices will have come about because of fear. Fear is the underlying, hidden reason for every evil action, every evil thought, and every evil state-of-being. Yet, ironically, most people don't even realize that they are constantly living in this state of fear. It is hidden; it "*lies at the door*" to every decision we make (Gen. 4:7). It trips us up, yet it *lies down*, so we don't see that it is there. We become so distracted by the noise of outward living that we are not tuned into our reason for doing what we do. By extension, we are not tuned into the emotional turmoil that lies in the hidden realm of our subconscious.

To some degree, these fears are all based on lies. Fear of *anything* (that is, anything other than the overwhelming experience of the Infinite Power of God) is not based on truth. In fact, through fear we begin to turn things inside-out in our thinking, and in our interactions with the world.

It is of great significance that Eve looked at the *forbidden fruit* and desired the wisdom that she believed would come from eating it. In many ways, this is so very absurd. She already had access to *infinite wisdom* in her relationship with the One in Whom all true wisdom lies. Her personal access to wisdom was always at hand; being found within her own person through connection to God. She was made in the image and likeness of her God. She was a daughter of the Creator of everything, the Creator Who knows everything. His Presence was *inside* of her since the very moment she was brought forth into the world. She was a part of His family, and He was a part of her. Yet, she sought for wisdom *outside* of herself. This outward wisdom could never be the true wisdom that she already had within her most holy, inward place.

Because she began to run after something outside of herself - which she already had within - Eve was disconnecting herself from her own inward being. She was essentially tearing her physical self away from her true Spiritual self. This tear would become the mortal wound that would lead to death. This, then, is the very reason that eating from the *Tree of the Knowledge of Good and Evil* would bring death. And in subsequent generations, after the same error of the progenitors of humanity, we have all learned to eat from this same tree - seeking outward satisfaction for that which can only be authentically found within. Consequently, ever since, all of humanity has become fractured in each of our persons. We have become misaligned in the sense that there is an inner breach, or mortal wound, between our present physical existence and our true Spiritual, inward selves.

In some mysterious way, our Spiritual self is still there, yet our awareness has been distanced from the truth of this real, holistic *us*. We keep our attention focusing outside of ourselves. And there is much constant, external noise to keep us attracted to that external counterfeit experience. One strong source of this external noise comes in various forms of religious participation, much of which creates a *feeling* of Divine connection. Yet, very often this is a pseudo-experience. In this case, while it may mimic the real experience of connecting to Divine-consciousness, what people are actually experiencing is an *outward*, collective, human-consciousness.

Distorted human-consciousness conceives of its own version of the Divine, and this becomes the foundation for shared false belief systems; ultimately associated with a definitive, limited view of God. Of course, the world is full of man-made religious constructs that bring illness, and do not serve to help us to reconnect with the potential of our true, inward, Spiritual selves. These outward pseudo-spiritual experiences do not promote true connection with the Divine Being Who made us in the first place, but often get in the way of our relationship with the Creator.

Moreover, society is brimming with the distraction of noise of all kinds. In a multiplicity of ways, our cultural norms are centered upon interacting around this noise. Entertainment, constant eating, stimulants, gossiping, fretting over social challenges, religiously-based activities, conflict within religious circles, theological arguments, fear-based news, addictions of all kinds, parties, coffee shops, movies, reality TV, night clubs, etc. – these are all part of the external noise that keeps us reeling outside of ourselves. Of course, a number of these things are not necessarily "bad" in and of themselves, but added up together, distracted living can prevent human beings from ever reconnecting with who they really are. Like caged animals running around in the external enclosure they have been locked up in, people can easily go in circles. Emotional frustrations and pain; mixed with distraction, temporary pleasures and entertainment; keep people on the move without ever really getting anywhere. Without a doubt, this is a recipe for becoming worn and broken creatures, rather than reaching the glorious heights for which we were originally created.

So how do we break out of all of this circular insanity?

In reality, it is beautifully simple. It is by seeking the Creator, getting to know Him, and learning to completely trust in Him while simultaneously *letting go of all fear*. Deep down, each of us knows the Creator is there for us. We just need to let go of the idea that His love for us is somehow attached to a particular religious sect. If we seek Him in truth and sincerity, we concurrently need to let go of the apprehension that He will let us fail in the end. We need to discard the fear that we will become "fallen" in our very efforts to seek Him. This latter point is so important chiefly because, in so many ways throughout religious history, people have been aggressively programmed into this doubt-filled perception concerning the Divine.

The simple truth is that God is found *beyond* the context of every man-made, rigid, boxed, religiously-derived system. Many have been emphatically taught that if they leave the religious system to which they belong, they will be doomed to destruction. The truth is - since He cannot be found within those very constructs - we *must* leave behind a fearful, absolute commitment to these fixed belief systems, or we may never find Him in fullness.

Through my own personal life experience I have found that by walking away from man-made constrictions to seek the Eternal Creator, I have become freed-up to begin a beautiful journey into a glorious unknown reality. Along the way I have had the opportunity to face up to the ideas I had been taught earlier in life, and have gradually shed the false beliefs I once believed to be true.

Since many of these beliefs become a part of our subconscious, this process can take time; nevertheless, the main thing is that the Creator is there to help us in the process. This is the *wilderness journey* that each of us needs to embark on, in some form or another, and it undoubtedly comes with its challenges. Yet these particular challenges are beautifully intended to create amazing growth for us, while humbling us at the same time. This process changes us into someone far different than who we were when we first began. And what we become in this life, as His people, makes this educational growth-period both valuable and necessary. Furthermore, the wisdom we gain, as Proverbs instructs us, is worth more than all the material treasures in the world.

Another relevant point that is interesting and valuable to note, as shared by Solomon in the Biblical Proverbs, is that it is not good to have a bonded-servant to "reign."

> *"Luxury is not fitting for a fool;* ***much less for a slave to rule over princes.****"* (Pro. 19:10)

Perhaps this may not seem fair at first. In reality, however, it is simply because he has not gained the wisdom required; he has not been adequately trained as a leader. Consequently, the *wilderness-process* is the training of the Almighty Creator: taking us out of bondage and then vigorously training us to become true, loving, righteous, humble leaders who put their trust in Him. This is how we will become miraculously fit for the remarkable role that He has planned for each of us.

The God that I have come to know doesn't reside in any construct made by men. But I do believe that He has revealed important Divine truths in the Hebrew writings of old, with its foundation being the five books written by Moses, known as the Torah. Through my own Spiritual journey, I have found that these foundational teachings, in their original Hebrew form, are eternal and infinite in their educational essence. The truths found there, once we tune into them, will be repeatedly reconfirmed. It is these truths that are hidden to those who still cling to the man-made constructs and perspectives that they have been taught. In other words, these hidden insights are the glory of the One True God, which He will reveal to those who are truly looking for Him in sincerity, and who are willing to go to any length to find Him.

Because humankind has been living in a world that is decidedly *outside of the garden*, the ensuing trend has been the subsequent manufacturing of all kinds of religious ideas and products that are very much apart from the True God. These inaccurate, humanly-conceived concepts are also apart from our true nature, our true selves, and the Spiritual element of our created being. While there are valuable, intrinsic truths incorporated into many of the world's religions to varying degrees, there is likewise an array of problematic errors also commonly found therein.

Many of these religious errors have similarities that come from the same dysfunctional foundation. Because of the common experience of disconnection from our true, inward self, and due to our innate, intense desire to reconnect with our true essence, we are consequently attracted to religions that have the tendency to *externalize* Spiritual elements of ourselves: elements which we already have within. This externalized spirituality is a false, primary ingredient found within the religious sphere. And, though outward connection is attractive and familiar, it can never satisfy. The most problematic element of this pseudo-connection is that it keeps people looking for the Divine on the *outside*, and we can never deeply connect with the Creator there. On many levels therefore, these religious belief-systems bear the insanely ironic potential to keep us *away from* the True Creator.

In like manner, many religions labor to externalize the inward, personal turmoil that humans commonly experience, and then methodically fixate that pain outwardly onto another "Divine" figure so that the members, *mistakenly,* don't realize their real need to face it within their own person. There is a tendency to religiously and subconsciously see our own struggle *out there* in some external story, and never be motivated to introspectively understand the true Divine purpose of our life challenges.

Because of the fact that genuine elements of our *inward* selves are *outwardly* reflected in common religious concepts, these ideas end up feeling strikingly familiar to people.

These outward religious concepts *seem* true, and we can feel a sense of personal connection with them. This, then, is the challenge that we all need to come to terms with: being able to discern *ultimate truth* from that which feels *familiar*. This is the reason that so many have worshipped gods in the form of men, over the millennia. Somehow we realize there is a Divine potential inside of ourselves that we intrinsically desire to connect with; yet, we may also be considerably distanced from it in our awareness. Unfortunately, these man-made forms of religious worship do not help us to connect with the Divine Consciousness at the core of who we are. In fact, religious falsity relentlessly keeps us outside of ourselves, and distanced from the greater potential within, which we long to be manifesting in our lives.

Most significantly, false religions promise to "reconnect us" with the Divine. And it is precisely because of this manufactured assurance of reconciliation that we can end up seeking for the externalized mediatorship of religion – of authorities – of sages – of saviors – of teachers – of priests – of rabbis – of pastors – of gurus – of kings – of mighty ones – of God's 'representatives' – for the sake of securing what many have come to believe is *salvation*. Of course, I am not suggesting that we cannot benefit from the mentorship of individuals who have something of value to offer, including those who lead in the context of the Spiritual realm. Problems arise, however, when we start looking to men for *all* the answers, thereby ignoring our primary need to look to our Creator for guidance, asking Him to help us discover *Who He really Is.*

The reality is, that our reconnection to God does not come through external, religious mediators. Connection to the

Divine was given to us long ago; it was the foundational gift that God gave to us - intrinsically akin to *who we are*. In order to reconnect with the Divine, we simply need to reconnect with who we were created to be at the very beginning. We need to go back to our beginnings and shed millennia of messy falsities and lying fears. We need to stop *seeking for a king* as our ancestors have done for thousands of years, and start connecting to the King *that we already have*. That is, *The King of the Universe*, Who has actually invited us to rule with Him, and has gorgeously designed us for this very role.

We were created to have direct access to our God. We were created to have direct communion. And as the story of the two trees in Eden powerfully indicates, it is a wholesale lie that wisdom, fulfillment, and Divine appointment come from another source within the created world. While the pseudo-religions of men do provide an experience of comfort, they can never ultimately bring the genuine reconnection that comes by seeking the transformational ways of the Creator Himself.

The amazing thing about the Hebrew writings is that in their pure, unbiased form they are perfectly harmonious with the created world. They beautifully assist us in tuning into the mysteries of the physical creation. And, aligning with the design of the Creator brings us so much closer to Him. The universal laws and ways of the Creator truly elevate us. They help us to become what we were made to be: alike to the Divine, as refined, connected, enriched, fully-enlivened, and beautifully transcendent *human-beings*.

4

The Serpent Mediator

The Genesis record shows us that the very first mediator between God and men was *the serpent* in the garden.

Of course, he was by no means a mediator appointed by God, but rather a self-appointed, false mediator who claimed to understand God's "real" intentions. Eve, as we already know, having lost touch with her internal trust of the Creator, began to look *outside* of herself; ultimately deferring her authority to the lying mediatorship of the Serpent, who spoke with authority. This serpent spoke authoritatively, as though he *really knew* what God was all about, all the while speaking in opposition to what God *actually said*. "*For God knows…*" says the serpent. He asserts himself as if he has an exclusive, inside knowledge about some enigmatical objective of the Divine. In this vein, he places himself, as well as his reasoning, between Eve and her Creator.

Before we dig any deeper on this topic, let's balance some details concerning what we are to understand about *who* or *what* this serpent actually *is*. Fittingly, leaving aside all of the religious controversy and theological surmising about the nature of the serpent, for clarification we will seek to simply deal with the text itself.

The Hebrew word for serpent - *"nachash"* - is actually very interesting. In Hebrew, we find that *nachash* means *"to hiss, or whisper,"* which is fascinating because this definition is reminiscent (and representative as well) of the constant *external noise* we are bombarded with, consistently, throughout our lives.[3] It is no surprise, then, that this noise carries influence over our personal subconscious. From the time we are born, our environment is full of this persistent *"hissing,"* which comes from the *externally-focused* consciousness of humankind. It is a reverberation that permeates the world around us. By extension, all of this serpentine noise is rooted in the fears and doubts that are coming from the pain of humanity's disconnection from God, and a detachment from a perfect trust in Him.

Connecting some new details, now, with what we have already reviewed, here are a few specifics associated with this particular serpent:

- The serpent questions Eve.

- The serpent begins his dialogue with Eve by referencing God's initial commandment: *"Has God indeed said, 'You shall not eat from any tree of the garden?'"* This opening gave Eve the opportunity to remember the original commandment of God.

> In this sense, the question of the serpent served as a test of Eve's commitment to the *precise words* of her Creator. She only needed to finish the quoted words of God in her exchange with the Serpent. Instead, she responded with the *altered version* of His law, as we have been considering.

- The serpent responds to Eve's *altered truth* with an *altered truth* of his own, thereby continuing to contradict what they were Divinely told. He claims that they would *not die* after eating, but would instead be "*like gods (or elohim), having opened eyes, and knowing good and evil.*"

> What exactly are the "*opened eyes*" that the serpent promised? Adam and Eve already had access to the primary Source of wisdom, having been designed to connect to the Divine Consciousness in a very close and intimate way, within the very core of their being. The *opened eyes* introduced by the Serpent, however, would bring about a new state of affairs altogether, wherein they would be using their *eyes* in order to *hunt* for wisdom. In other words, they would enter into a state in which they would always be seeking for knowledge and satisfaction *outside of themselves*. They would be pursuing the things of life from a source

they could *visibly* rely upon, rather than operating with Spiritual insight. In this way, humanity would become disconnected from the awareness that the genuine key to *who we are* already lies on the inside – in the invisible realm – and within the original human blueprint. The act of eating from the forbidden tree would perilously serve to push generations of humanity outside of themselves, and divide the human race from its very core existence. A cursory glance over our past history is enough to demonstrate that we have been disparagingly torn from ourselves, and painfully broken up. It is no wonder that this reality would ultimately bring death into the world.

- Eve makes the claim that the serpent deceived her (Gen. 3:13).

    > *"And YHWH God said to the woman,*
    > *'What is this you have done?'*
    > *The woman said, 'The serpent deceived me,*
    > *and I ate.'"*

- YHWH makes this declaration against the serpent (Gen. 3:14-15).

    > *"Because you have done this,*
    > *You are cursed more than all cattle,*
    > *And more than every beast of the field;*
    > *On your belly you shall go,*
    > *And you shall eat dust*

All the days of your life.
And I will put enmity
Between you and the woman,
And between your seed and her seed;
He shall bruise your head,
And you shall bruise his heel."

With these points in mind, let's explore the Biblical record a little deeper so that we can better understand this serpent. Again, we'll seek to do this with prayerful consideration, without getting side-tracked by various predetermined beliefs about it.

In the early Genesis narrative, we are given an extensively important and valuable truth. This truth, as it turns out, indicates that our expectation and anticipation have the potential to become eventual realities. As being *"like"* God and *"in His image,"* in a mysterious and amazing way, we were made to be creators of the very reality that will play out before us, in our lives. This is because the Creator fashioned us to have the elevated capacity to work with Him, and to be a part of His glorious family. In this sense, just as God consciously *intended and expected* to bring about the reality of this creation, so too we have the unseen power to manifest our *thoughts and expectations* (our focused consciousness) into reality.

In the case of the fall in the garden, Adam and Eve believed that they were in grave danger of *falling prey* to becoming eaters of this tree. Essentially, that's the primary reason they created the additional commandment. They did so, acting as though they were likely going to become victims of this tree, and consequently believed themselves to be at great risk.

These are all false beliefs. The remarkable thing about all of this is that once they began to believe and internalize these false beliefs, their postulations became manifested into their reality in a very real and tangible way. They believed they were at great risk of becoming eaters of this "deadly" tree: and so they did, thereby becoming victims of their own anticipated, self-fulfilling failure. Accordingly, when faced with the serpent, Eve's fear-based reasoning led her to quickly give in to the noisy stimulus being hissed towards her, and she found herself doing the one thing that they had tried so hard to avoid.

The very fact that Adam and Eve added to the instruction that God gave them demonstrates that they were *anticipating failure*, and were subsequently seeking to protect against it through their own means. Fear, however, could never be satisfied with these means, since the dread of failure is apart from the eternal refuge of trust and truth. Even after they created the supposed "safeguard" of adding to the Divine Law, the confusion of fear still remained. It, therefore, ensues in the Genesis narrative, that Eve completely forgets the details concerning what the original instruction actually was, and alternatively comes to believe a lie that they had created themselves. Namely, that not only would they die if they *ate* from the tree, but that they would die if they even *touched* the tree. It is only because of their anticipation of failure that they added a new aspect to God's law. This was not a safeguard – it just fueled their fear of failing.

Ultimately, their fear-based anticipation of failure does become their reality, as we see unfold. The *lie* itself, finding conception in their own minds, ultimately brought forth the *manifestation of lying* into their physical midst; becoming a polluting force in the environment they were living in. In the Genesis account, the manifestation of lying is seen in the figure of the serpent itself. In this way, the events here point to the astonishing concept that, somehow, the serpent was a *creation* of Adam and Eve, and not a natural element of God's original creation. The mechanism for how *exactly* human conception becomes reality, no one can really say. Yet, it has been observed that our ability to create our own reality is mysteriously related to the universal *Law of Vibration* (aka. the Law of Attraction).

Now, it is a pretty massive assertion that I have just made. The serpent created by Adam and Eve? *What*? How on earth can I presume this to be the case? Again, I refer solely to the text itself as the source of this conclusion. As we shall see, the majestic simplicity of the Genesis text actually does lend support to this concept.

Please note that I am neither claiming that they necessarily literally "formed and made" the serpent in a physical sense, nor that God had no physical part to play. Exactly what the mechanism was in the creation of the serpent, and the role that God played in the bringing forth of the serpent, we're not told in Genesis (and I, personally, am not presuming to know). We also don't know for sure if the Genesis serpent was a literal, physical being or purely figurative, for that matter.

Since we are unaware of the intrinsic capabilities of Adam and Eve before their *fall*, it is possible that they would have had the incredible ability to influence reality to the extent of creating an entirely new, *literal* creature. Alternatively, another hypothesis relating to the possibility of there having been a *literal serpent* who spoke with Eve, is such that it may have already been created along with the rest of the animal kingdom on the sixth day of creation, and then afterwards, Adam and Eve's fearful vibration could have influenced an altered distortion in the animal's consciousness. At that point, it would begin to literally embody a changed, false perception. Hence, when the serpent speaks, he mirrors back to Eve the distortion of her own making.

On the other hand, if the serpent was purely *figurative*, we see from this viewpoint the possibility that the serpent was simply a specially-selected, Biblical *symbol* to represent the negative manifestation of fear-based reality. It is this reality that Adam and Eve had brought into their environment through the vibrational energy of their own fearful conception.

Whichever the case may be, as I mentioned before, even though it has been the subject of much debate over the years, we don't ultimately know whether the early events in Genesis are literal or allegorical in nature. In all likelihood, this is a question that actually doesn't matter. For those of us who believe in the Divine inspiration of Genesis, either way, these details accurately represent the truth of what happened, in perfect essence. What matters is discovering the ultimate truth that this narrative is pointing us to. Quite simply, the heart of the matter is that we hear, and be transformed by, the message inherent in these things.

In this early setting, depicted in the Genesis beginning, we are being Divinely instructed concerning the outplay of universal truth. I'd venture to say that this is always the most valuable element, and primary purpose, of the

Scriptures. With that in mind, let's continue on in this vein: seeking to find what is being revealed to us in the details concerning the serpent's appearance on the scene.

First of all, the opening of Genesis chapter three indicates that the serpent was probably not an original element of the creation – or at least, not in the manner of its distorted nature seen in the events in this chapter.

> "*Now the serpent was more cunning **than any beast** of the field which **YHWH God had made**.*" (Gen. 3:1)

The very way the serpent is introduced to us is through the above sentence, wherein we are told that this serpent was more cunning *than any of the beasts that God had made*. What it does not say (even in the original Hebrew), is that the serpent was more cunning than any "*other*" beast that YHWH had made. The narrative is specifically telling us that this serpent was somehow separate, and different, from the nature of any of the animals that God had made. At the very least, this leaves the possibility that this particular serpent was not made according to the original intent or creation of God at all. Its troublesome nature, as indicated in Genesis chapter three, was not part of the creation that the Creator declared to be "*very good.*"

Secondly, the word for "*cunning,*" as we see here in the English translation, is directly tied to Adam and Eve. To observe this properly, we need to look at the Hebrew text itself. I'll explain as follows:

The Hebrew root word for "*cunning*" shares the same root wording as "*naked.*" As we recall, being *naked* was the original state of Adam and Eve at the beginning of creation.

> *"And they were both **naked**, the man and his wife, and were not ashamed." (Gen. 2:25)*

- The Hebrew word for *"naked"* is *"'arowm."*
- The Hebrew word for *"cunning"* is *"`aruwm."*
- Both words come from the root *"`aram."*
    - → *"`Aram"* carries the meaning of *"uncovering"* or *"making bare."*

What does all of this mean? Here are my suggestions:

We see that Adam and Eve are *"naked"* and not ashamed. They are *"uncovered,"* which meant that their bare state is one in which there was nothing for them to feel ashamed of, when viewed openly. They had nothing to hide since their true person was pure, balanced, and healthful.

Then, at some point after Adam and Eve's amending of the commandment regarding the tree, along came this serpent who was *"'aruwm"* (*cunning*). Though *aruwm* is often translated into English as 'subtle' or 'cunning,' its meaning is actually in line with the concept of *uncovering*. In other words, the serpent was a mechanism by which Adam and Eve would become *uncovered* in their new state of fear. Though they had already developed the grievous mentality of fear, the seriousness of this fear-based mindset was not yet uncovered or made bare until the serpent had successfully convinced Eve to disregard the commandment outright, and eat of the forbidden tree. This demonstrates that it was their underlying fears that made them susceptible to the serpent's deceitful influence. This is why it could be said that the serpent was acting as a type of mirror for their disguised fears, reflecting their anticipation of failure.

I'm not suggesting that the serpent was, therefore, a good thing, necessarily. I believe the text indicates otherwise, as we see that through the adverse creative-process of Adam and Eve's fear-based, false beliefs, the serpent was a component part of the evil that became their very reality. In other words, the serpent was the manifestation of their fear-based lies, distrust, and overall state of imbalance. Because of this, Adam and Eve became ensnared in their own trap – resulting in the painful course of sin and death that came into the world.

To put it more directly, the serpent - in some way - *is* their fear. It is fear's outward manifestation. The man and the woman feared the forbidden tree; they feared that they would fail to keep God's commandment; and their fear evidently became reality through the medium of the serpent. The circumstance of the serpent leading them to failure was simply their fearful anticipation, playing out into reality. This whole scenario was created by Adam and Eve who, rather than simply *trusting God* and *guarding His words*, had lost touch with their certainty of success through Him. It was through this devastating disconnection with their Creator that the focus of their thoughts became crystallized into a fear of failure, and of the tree itself. Amazingly (and sadly), this all became their reality.

If Eve had recognized the serpent for what it was, it's certainly possible that she could have rejected the lying reasoning that the creature was presenting to her. However, because of her own confused mind, and also because of the lies she had begun to believe, truth itself became difficult to discern. Furthermore, had she turned to God at this point, there is no doubt He would have helped her. Sadly though, trust in the Creator had been laid aside, occasioning the calamity that would ensue.

Another valuable lesson in relation to these events concerns the nature of *fear-based decision-making*. That is, fear-based decisions are strikingly restrictive in nature. This is true whether they are characteristically "*conservative*" decisions, or "*liberal*" ones. In the garden, the human-invented commandment which directed Adam and Eve *not to even touch this tree* prevented the complete God-given freedom of movement that they were originally endowed with. What this also meant was that the pleasure associated with being *free* was no longer their experience.

As we are well aware of today, a lack of true joy leaves a void in the spirit: a void that people attempt to fill with temporary pleasure-seeking activities. At best, this can only distract the person, allowing them to momentarily forget that they are deprived of genuine, lasting happiness. This sense of intense emptiness will never authentically be filled with external distractions, and thus people enter into the vicious cycle of forever pursuing outward stimulation until the very last day of their life, or until they eventually come to the realization that there is another way to true fulfillment.

When the serpent appears on the scene and presents the *Tree of the Knowledge of Good and Evil* in a new way, Eve begins to distortedly see it as a way out of the painfully restrictive life she had already created for herself. In all likelihood, she had come to desire throwing-off the shackles that she now wore, probably even mistaking them for the shackles *of God*. In this she misinterpreted her situation, since her true need was to reconnect with her trust in the Divine. Only trust would be the means by which she would *truly* rid herself of her own self-created, loathsome restraints.

With distorted vision, Eve altered her view of the forbidden tree and began to perceive it as something that was *"good for food, pleasant to the eyes, and desirable to make one wise."* What Eve intrinsically desired was the freedom, joy and pleasure that came from reconnecting with God and His gorgeously freeing ways, but she inadvertently began to mistake the *Tree of the Knowledge of Good and Evil* as being the source of those things instead. In the end, she set aside the simplicity of God's original command and, to her peril, chose a false reality over ultimate truth.

So, what is being deeply communicated *to us* through these ancient words?

Principally, it is imperative for us to understand that *fear kills* us. Fear leads us down the wrong roads. Fear blocks life. Fear is based on lies. By fear, we forget *truth*. Our personal fears become manifested into reality in our lives in some way, creating a vicious cycle that destroys us, as well as our potential.

Fear is our singular great enemy. Yet, strangely, we are the ones who create the fears that we cling to. In this way, we inadvertently *give-power*, *permit*, and *enable* our fears: by developing the false belief that whatever we fear has legitimate power over us. Furthermore, because we have such creative power through our thoughts, our fear-based thinking creates all kinds of malady and destruction in the world.

This has been the reality of humanity for millennia now.

It is scientifically fitting that the Scriptures depict fear as a *serpent*, which, of course, is a *base reptile*. In terms of our physical brain structure, scientists have noted that the brainstem and cerebellum are both parts of our neuroanatomy that are considerably *reptilian* in design.[4] Among other things, this is a reactive part of our brain that is shared by humans and other animals: even including various forms of reptiles. Appropriately, these brain structures are associated with the *stress response* and, accordingly, are triggered by various fear stimulants. Generally speaking, this part of our nervous system is highly reactive in nature and is closely associated with impulsive, automatic, reactive behaviours.

The brainstem and cerebellum are essential, advantageous parts of the brain when it comes to putting our body into action with the *fight, flight* or *freeze* responses whenever needed (like when we have to run from a burning building). Yet we have been altogether programmed to allow this part of our brain to *govern* us, instead of actually *serving* us. Consequently, our experience of life has become saturated with chronic fear and the limiting beliefs that accompany it. Instead of wisely discerning the signals being sent by the brain (through tools of Spiritual intuition and higher thinking), we have instead learned the sorry practice of bowing down under the reactive thought processes that those signals have triggered. In some senses, we have allowed the signals to gain the rule over us. Looking at it from a decidedly more macro-social perspective, this common human reactive-mode also provides the fodder for ruling parties to gain the advantage over other population groups, by deliberately triggering fear pathways through the promotion of collective ideologies and dogmas.

A significant scientific point with all of this is that the stress response shuts down higher reasoning centers in the brain in order to shunt blood to wherever it is needed (such as our limbs). In tandem with this natural phenomenon is the subsequent inactivation of the frontal cortex: the element of the human brain which many scientists and researchers regard as the part of our brain that physically makes us the most "human." Without belabouring the point here, the frontal cortex is what sets our neurological intelligence, and intellectual capacity, apart from all other creatures in the earth's realm.

The manner in which most people have been brought up in the world promotes a mindset that causes them to be highly reactive in daily decision making, as well as in general interactions with one another. While this conditioning allows the cogs and gears of civilization to keep on turning, it also sets the stage for humans to be detached from their true ability to think and reason in a highly intelligent (and authentic) manner.

It is also imperative to realize that our brain is not the place of our true identity. Our true-self is *above* the brain, according to the miracle of our original design. Essentially the Divine design of the human being was such that, our brain was marvelously created to be an amazingly powerful *physical* organ, wherein the spiritual-self was intended to be its *driver,* not it's submissive passenger.

Putting it one way, we are gifted with the spiritual capacity to be in command of our brain. This is so important to understand because, unless we skillfully learn to take the wheel of our thinking, we are sure to be driven *right off the road*! Governing our brain is a fundamental aspect of learning to become the leader that we were created to be. True leadership starts with wisely ruling over our own physical self, according to the original blueprint of the Creator. What this means is that we need to be a pursuer of substantial wisdom, understanding and insight concerning our design, and how various parts of our body work. This includes coming to an in-depth understanding concerning the structure and function of the human brain.

The Biblical "*seed of the serpent*" can be seen as those who are driven by lower levels of thinking and fear-based reactivity, rather than intelligence and wisdom. For millennia this has included virtually *all of humanity*, to some degree or another. This base, reactive mindset is the conventional norm that we have each been taught to manifest, and human civilization has evolved into a virtual collective of these manifestations. Thankfully, however, our Creator is calling us to something more. In the words of Genesis, our calling is to become the "*seed of the woman.*" Or, in other words, it is to become the *human-being* we were always intended to be.

Though they will have been plagued by the reptilian brain throughout history, the heritage of the *seed of the woman* is that they will ultimately get in tune with higher levels of thinking, and thereby put reactive, fearful reasoning in its place. They will crush the mindset (the "head") of the serpent, with the new awareness that the rulership of reactive thinking no longer has any place within their person. This is *key* to understanding the nature of the calling: to become a part of God's collective family. By stepping into higher levels of consciousness, we will finally be fitted to effectively, and lovingly, govern over all that God has put into our care. This is the means by which healing will spring up in the earth, and all of the earth will be filled by God's amazing glory.

> *"But as truly as I live, all the earth shall be filled with the glory of YHWH."* (Num. 14:21)

After the expulsion of Adam and Eve from the garden, in the very next chapter (Gen. 4) we see that the seed of the serpent mindset has already infiltrated their family. The reactivity of Cain shatters family congeniality and leads to the very first murder. In this narrative there is also invaluable instruction for us, in order to help facilitate our ability to rise above the base mind.

> *"If you do well, will you not be accepted? And if you do not do well, sin lies at the door. And its desire is for you, but **you should rule over it**."* (Gen. 4:7)

As we see in the above quotation, God is reminding Cain that he does have the God-given capacity to rule over the reactive brain that has been triggered by the events preceding this verse.

Earlier in the chapter, we were told of the story of two separate offerings. One offering was given by Cain, and the other by his younger brother, Abel. We are then told of the fact that, because of the nature of each, God took notice of Abel's offering but not of Cain's. Because of this, Cain's anger was triggered, and he developed a highly reactive spirit. In the words of Genesis chapter four, *"Cain was very angry, and his countenance fell."*

Because Cain's reactive mind was triggered, God intervenes by offering him the above instruction. In this way, he was being educated to become aware of the fact that "sin" was lying down at the door, and eagerly ready to trip him up in his path. God also encourages Cain that: even though this was the case, Cain did have the capacity to *rule over it*. Thus, this plainly spells out for us that Cain was *not* his reactive mind. He was not his anger. The true-self is the one who is made *above* the thoughts that are generated from our own brain, and one who transcends the mentality that is promulgated in the external world. When we get in touch with this higher self, we come to understand how, in our true essence, we are actually the observant governor over the basic things that arise in our physical experience. Essentially, we were made to rule the physical brain, and not be ruled over by it.

In this case, we know that Cain had the ability to stop and consider. Had he been dwelling in a state of trust (rather than fear), he would have been ready and willing to consider the "why" in terms of God's not accepting his offering. He would have believed in the Love of the Creator, and understood that in all of our interactions with the Divine, God only wants what is best *for us*. But, Cain did not have his mind on those higher thoughts. His heart was not connected to God's love. Instead, his anger was triggered, and he allowed it to completely rule over him. This anger festered in his spirit and completely overwhelmed his person. He came to believe in the reasoning that the anger triggered in his brain, instead of believing in transcendent, universal truths. And this false reasoning eventually degraded him to the point that it brought death into his family, and forced him further away from the Divine Presence.

This is a sad and shocking turn of events. It is written so that we can recognize the unstable tendency we were born into, and so make better choices in our personal lives. We can become the one who connects with the exalted Consciousness of the Divine. This begins with awareness concerning our true-self. It begins when we connect with our true-self, and see that we are more than our physicality. We are more than the thoughts that arise in our heads and the dogmas that we have been fed.

In this story, we are being given a glimpse into how our personal responses, and the condition of our thoughts, play a direct role in the unfolding of our lives, and into whether or not we are a blessing to others, or otherwise, a curse. The promise of Genesis chapter four extends also to us, in that even though "*sin lies at the door*" when we get off track in our lives, there is opportunity for us to become masters over it.

We can take courage that we can become the master of every false fear residing in our person. Many of those fears are so ingrained in society that we may not even realize they are there. They have become programmed into the fabric of our overall perspective, and the way we view the world. We assume them to be *truth* when, in fact, they are wholly *untrue*.

Very much so, we can become the *"seed of the woman"* who crushes the mind of the serpent. We can rule over fear, and the lies associated with the common fears of the world. In fact, it's actually our Divine calling to do so. Fear, and the damaging manifestation of it, is a primary destructive force in the earth. Through higher consciousness we can rise above it, no longer being held captive under its false pretenses. And we can assist others to do the same.

God is calling us to bravery. He has encouraged us to believe. He has summoned us to victory – in the face of every fear.

"Have I not commanded you? Be strong and courageous. Do not be afraid; do not be discouraged, for YHWH your God will be with you wherever you go." (Jos. 1:9)

5

The Essence of Leadership

To fill the common void of anxious doubt within ourselves, there is only one authentic solution: we must simply trust God.

Likewise, the seriousness of distrust can be Biblically demonstrated by the fact that this was the underlying catalyst for the very first murder recorded. In Genesis four, *Abel* was murdered by his brother *Cain*; yet even before the murder ensued, it is clear that Cain was manifesting a scarcity mindset, even in his interactions with the Divine.

As the Genesis record indicates, although Abel brought the *"firstborn"* of his flock, Cain only brought *"of his produce,"* and not the actual firstfruits themselves.[5] By bringing the best of our increase, it also means that we trust that God will bring an overflowing abundance of goodness into our lives. Additionally, when we lovingly bring the best of our firstfruits to God, it also serves to remind us that our Creator is the source of every good blessing in our lives. In fact, as we all know, He is the source of our *very life*. This seems like such an obvious statement, yet so often the turbulent mindset of fear manages to obscure this beautiful truth, preventing us from acting in accordance with this basic understanding.

> *"Honor YHWH with your wealth, and with the firstfruits of all your increase."* (Pro. 3:9)

On par with humanity's ancient errors in the garden, humankind has followed suit in so many ways. Similar to Adam and Eve allowing themselves to become controlled and ensnared by their fears, so too has the dominance of fear become an underlying experience of every society, ever since.

Whatever its form, fear has an ugly power in our lives in that it compels us to cling to things that we are not served by: things which are founded upon toxic beliefs and manufactured truths. Throughout history, fears have played a foundational role in the various ways that civilizations have functioned. Similarly, countless social organizations have been formed in such a way that parallels the particular fears residing in the collective consciousness of each generation. Quite frequently, it is fear that has fueled the formation of various institutions in the first place. In this sense, these man-made systems, down through time, have been patterned after the distorted mindset that we have inherited from Adam and Eve. Because the mindset we have collectively manifested is one which disconnects us from God, in the same way that Adam and Eve were banished from the Garden of His Presence, a particular pattern of behavior has since been repeated, generation after generation.

When we dwell outside of trust in the One Who made us, we are entering into a personal state of fear. Because of the discomfort of this fearful state, there is the human tendency to create our own *semblance of safety*, even though it is not genuine. It goes without saying that, as a part of our mysterious, exalted design, we long for a Spiritual connection. When people dwell in fear rather than a place of trust, however, they end up creating their own pseudo-spirituality that addictively allows them to feel safe, even if for only fleeting moments at a time. Naturally, this is quite different than the genuine, steadfast safety that is found in a true Spiritual connection with the Divine.

> *"To whom then will you liken God?*
> *Or what likeness will you compare to Him?*
> *The workman molds an image,*
> *The goldsmith overspreads it with gold,*
> *And the silversmith casts silver chains.*
> *'To whom then will you liken Me,*
> *Or to whom shall I be equal?' says the Holy One.*
> *Lift up your eyes on high,*
> *And see Who has created these things,*
> *Who brings out their host by number;*
> *He calls them all by name,*
> *By the greatness of His might*

> *And the strength of His power;*
> *Not one is missing."*
> (Isa. 40:18-19, 25-26)

Human history is replete with the image-making tendencies of humankind's altered nature. In a perpetual quest to find meaning in the often inexplicable phenomena that makes up our universe, it is very easy for us to compile constructs and 'likenesses' that we interpret to be of assistance to us in our navigation of what we don't easily understand.

Yet this pattern is often the behind-the-scenes reason for the formation of false religious-systems (or the willing, societal adherence to them). Not unlike Adam and Eve's demonstrated behavior in the Garden: within spiritual institutions, people can find it easy to unconsciously *add* to the simple instructions of our God as they seek to feel safe through these self-made *safety nets*. Moreover, each religion or denomination usually has its own recipe of religious doctrines and dogma, which they collectively consider to be *"The Ways of God."* In this manner, people begin to think that God is who they have *conceived Him to be*, rather than Who *He actually is*. Because this fear-based pattern of behavior has been repeating itself for millennia, the majority of humanity has almost completely lost track of His true nature and ways. Needless to say, this is also how idolatry entered into the world – and how the "Kingdoms of Men" came into being in the first place.

Since we were born to be leaders, and each of us was created to lovingly *"have dominion"* over the earth, then why are most people living as though they were born for little more than to be *cogs* in a system, ruled over by *other men*? Why have we become so convinced that we each have so very little access to power, personally, to do the *impossible*? Why do we fear stepping into the greatness that lies within? Why do we feel that it is good and right to be passive in our dealings with society – to be a *"nice person"* in a world wrought with injustice and unjust leadership? Do we have no responsibility for the state of the world? Are we really as powerless as we have been taught to believe? And finally, are we really at peace with staying safely nuzzled inside the tiny *comfort zones* that are collectively suffocating our true, intrinsic potential?

Many of us have been conditioned to believe that our primary spiritual-calling is to *"support"* the religious systems that we were brought up in. Many Biblically-oriented populations tend to assume that God will be the one to *do the rest*, in terms of bringing healing and restoration to the world. It is even frowned upon by some religious communities to even suggest that God actually *wants* us to do something about the state of the world, since they feel it is blasphemous to believe that people have *any power* to change the state of things in human affairs. Though I have often witnessed this behaviour among those of a Biblically-associated faith, these ideas are the epitome of absurdity when actually tested against the foundation of their own faith – the ancient Hebrew Scriptural record. Genesis, in fact, which is the book of beginnings, tells us the very opposite: teaching us that we were *Divinely intended* to be responsible for the earth, and everything that happens in it.

"So God created man in His own image; in the image of God He created him; male and female He created them. Then God blessed them, and God said to them, 'Be fruitful and multiply; ***fill the***

> ***earth** and **subdue it; have dominion** over the fish of the sea, over the birds of the air, and over every living thing that moves on the earth.'* (Gen. 1:27-28)

The Creator specifically tells Adam and Eve that their God-given role upon this earth was to be responsible for everything that happens upon it – *"fill the earth"* – *"subdue it"* – *"have rulership… over everything!"* Why, then, are the very people who believe in the authority of this book so quick to relinquish the responsibility that the Creator of the Universe has placed upon them? Furthermore, why would they call that a "Godly" way of looking at things? Is this not a glaring and striking contradiction?

"But that's just modern humanism" are the cries of some – when faced with the idea that we are called to take responsibility for the world's state of affairs. It is times such as these, where our God-given intelligence must consider the harder questions. As such, *is it* truly a shallow demonstration of mere humanism to consider our Divinely-appointed responsibility, or is it instead – literally – *from the Bible itself?* My personal perspective is that the Creator made us to rule, as His people. Rulership is the true nature of the human being. However, as I've outlined before, this calling is not to rule over other people. Rather, we are called to align ourselves with the One God, Who knows the unique leadership role for which we are each harmoniously fitted. Quite simply, every person is called to lead. Every single one of us has positions of leadership in which we will experience great joy in fulfilling. In order for this to become the reality of our life, we need simply to align ourselves with God so that we rule *with* Him. In turn, we will also cooperatively rule *with* each other.

The Creator never called us to rule alone. It is not a question of us *or* Him… it is us *with* Him. That's the way it was always supposed to be. We were made to be the *Prince With El* from the beginning, and were always intended to enjoy perfect Oneness in Him, as well as with one another, in His perfect order of things.

> *"For YHWH most high is worthy of awe; He is a great King over all the earth."* (Psalm 47:2)

When we think of *ruling*, most of us will probably think of rulership in the sense of humanity's traditional context of it: the political / monarchical versions that our species have known over the past several millennia. Most of us probably forget that there is even a place for rulership outside of men ruling over other men. This is because we have gotten so entrenched in the reality of human civilization being split up into *those in power* versus *those in servitude*. In the face of this broad categorization of things, we have forgotten that the earth is teeming with all kinds of *other life* needing our love, leadership, and care. We have been created to lead *together*, as loving servant-guardians, over the rich diversity of life upon the earth, and all within the context of a garden-like existence.

By God's original design, humanity was to have no form of authoritarian government whatsoever, excepting the Kingship of the Almighty Himself, Who is the author of our joyous freedom. This order of the universe gives rise to a genuine existence of fun, beauty, pleasure and joy. With the realization of the original blueprint of the Creator, we share ideas and talents, and we enjoy the fruit of each other's labours. This is the future world that God has promised to eventually bring about, and He has invited us to step up to the plate right now. It is only when we realize who we are and what we have been called to do, that the earth can gradually move forward in its ultimate destiny of being filled with His glory. The reason for this is that His glory corresponds with His perfect design, and we begin to attune to that design when we move into becoming the loving and harmonious leaders that we were born to be.

I recently had a compelling dream, which I believe complements the perspective that I am sharing here. I will endeavor to put it into words…

My dream opened up with a scenario wherein I was being sent to a quiet wilderness area, along with a camera, to do some photography. There was little plant-life in this area, and the land was open, and somewhat barren. As I looked around, observing my surroundings, I saw a lone buck in the distance. I was very interested in it and, naturally, felt compelled to take some photos. Yet before I had the chance to position the camera, my compulsion to photograph was overwhelmed by a stronger feeling that I didn't want to frighten it away. For some reason, I just wanted to keep my eyes locked on it instead: so I did. Over the next few moments I stood quietly and motionless, simply observing. To my very big surprise, before I knew it, the buck was approaching me. I had been standing on a small, elevated hill where I had a good view of the surroundings, and the buck kept moving closer until he finally approached the bottom of the hill where I was standing.

Gracefully and gently, he rose onto his hind legs and placed his front legs onto the steep slope of the hill, right at my feet. Almost instinctively, I found myself reaching out towards him. With my palm facing down, he responded by slowly raising his head toward my hand, and touching my palm with his soft nose. This all happened with a beauty, grace and steadiness that was quite overwhelming for me. Within a few brief moments of this incredible encounter, he then quietly and peacefully lowered himself back onto all four legs at the base of the hill.

I was awe-struck by this encounter, and while barely having a moment to properly reflect on what had just happened, another animal approached the scene. This time it was a full grown *rhinoceros*. Before I had much time to think about the fact that I was being approached by a very large and intimidating creature, the rhino – like the buck before it – also slowly and peacefully approached the hill and stood right next to the buck. Strangely enough, as the other animal had done he also began raising his body upon the edge of the hill. Again, I stretched my hand out in front of me with my palm facing down, and he too – with his immense horn arched back, out of the way - touched my palm with his nose. He then quietly lowered himself back down and went on his way. It was at this moment that I realized something very poignant; something which I was sure never to forget. These animals had just peacefully pledged allegiance to me. I was a leader to them, and they recognized me for this.

By this time in the dream, it was beginning to get dark and my thoughts began wandering to the fact that if I don't start heading back, it would soon be pitch-black and I would be stuck in this isolated area for the night. The thought unnerved me a little, prompting me to start making my way back to "civilization."

Interestingly, however, the buck had never left that spot; again, I became aware of his presence. He stood quietly, not making a move, and simply watched me as I began to leave. And it was in the quiet starkness of that moment that I became enormously overwhelmed by the sensation that he didn't understand why I felt such a strong need to leave. It made no sense to him that I wasn't just staying the night out there in nature. It occurred to me that, from his perspective, I was somehow supposed to be a part of that landscape.

This is when I woke up, and my immediate thought upon waking was *"Prince With El."* In some way, I believe this dream was a small glimpse of what God had intended for humanity from the very beginning.

For so long, we have been disconnected from our own role as leader in the earth. Yet, as Biblical believers, this concept of unique leadership roles for each person should not really come as a surprise to us. We are told about the fact that we were created for this very thing! Male and female: both were made to be a part of this leadership and, by extension, their generations after them. This is what it is to be *human*.

> *"So God created man in His own image; in the image of God He created him; male and female He created them. Then God blessed them, and God said to them, 'Be fruitful and multiply; fill the earth and subdue it; have dominion over the fish of the sea, over the birds of the air, and over every living thing that moves on the earth.'"*
> (Gen. 1:27-28)

The problem, according to our upbringing and all of its associated programming, is that we have altogether become unaware of what it means to be a human being, by design. Because of this, we go through the course of this life not acting like the soul that we are at our core – at least not to our God-given potential.

Humans were made to take care of the planet and all life upon it. We were created to live in a *garden world* as we clearly see evidenced in the design of the garden, where God placed the first couple to dwell. Of course, this kind of lifestyle involves constant interaction with the plant and animal life present there, and it necessarily involves consideration and care for the soil itself, from which all other life is nourished and fed.

> *"Whoever tends a fig tree will eat its fruit."* (Pro. 27:18)

> *"Whoever is righteous has regard for the life of his animal, but even the compassion of the wicked is cruel."* (Pro. 12:10)

As I believe we are all aware, humans have not acted like this since the 'fall,' as recorded in Genesis. Accordingly, humanity has not been experiencing life in a garden state. Not because it has not been a *possibility,* based on what is present in our environment, nor of our *ability*. Rather, humans have historically lived according to the strange tendency of herding into the man-made environments of cities, with much of the agriculture being owned by wealthy landowners who primarily produce agricultural 'products' to allow people to survive, yet not necessarily to thrive in the way God intended.

We also see historically, that humans have continually felt the need to have a *human director* over them: a king, an emperor, or the like. This is even despite the fact that most kings down through history have not looked after their subjects in a righteous manner. This is very strange, indeed, once we open our eyes to the fact that we were made to be leaders over wildlife and the rest of the creation *together*, as a *collective*. With this being the case, instead of connecting with our own humanity, we have become animal-like ourselves, seeking other humans to rule over us, as if we were the animals that needed human intervention for our wellbeing.

Don't get me wrong, though. I am not saying that we don't need each other – clearly God has taught us otherwise, and social science consistently confirms our need for healthy community.[6]

But, what is true community really supposed to look like? I believe that the Hebrew Scriptures are teaching us that a healthy community involves working together harmoniously, while personally taking on the special leadership role for which we were specifically and uniquely designed. Because of this, we have yet to see the full potential of community ultimately realized in our world, both socially and agriculturally. The full realization of this potential is really the essence of coming to be in tune with our Creator, while His perfect direction acts as our ethical compass.

> *"Make me know Your ways, O YHWH; teach me Your paths. Lead me in Your truth and teach me, for You are the God of my salvation; for You I wait all the day."* (Psa. 25:4-5)

Let's remember the following truth:

- The Creator is King.
- He has made us to be like Him, in His image: yet all of us are each completely unique manifestations.
- These manifested distinctions are extensions upon the earth of His Kingship and love.

If this is all true, what exactly does it mean? It is strange to think of the multifaceted diversity of planetary life, while also realizing that very few of us have gained much of an understanding concerning the universe's blueprint. It is also remarkable to consider the reality that everyone needs to be healthfully nourished by the food of God's fashioning, yet, in our day, very few of us know how to grow these things *at all*, let alone according to the best practices that are aligned with the design of the Creator.

To a large extent, even the world's farmers know very little about how to truly nourish the ground upon which they are farming. Even though there is much knowledge available today to be tapped into, still many of today's farmers do not cultivate with wisdom and understanding, respecting the intricacies of life that are present in healthy soil. Accordingly, they have no idea about how to promote the harmony of soil organisms, which are necessary to support the optimum healthfulness of the earth's produce. This is precisely why we have a world that is becoming flooded with GMO's and pesticides, since many farmers have been coaxed into these practices, specifically because of their lack of wisdom concerning the earth and its true needs.

Fortunately, however, many people are waking up to the fact that we need a better way. One of my favourite social trends in the world today is the *Permaculture* movement. The permaculture movement is essentially based upon a rich understanding of the intricacies of the natural world and how to create biodiversity to bring forth an abundance of food, in a wise and practical manner. It is truly beautiful and inspiring to see many of these permaculture gardens and organic farms, all specially and carefully designed to bring forth bountifully. These farms and gardens work *with* the natural laws of the Creator's design, rather than struggling *against* nature, as has been commonly experienced throughout agricultural history.

So let's just pause for a moment here, and take a quick trip back to the *Garden of Eden* in order to bring this all together.

Because of the fact that Adam and Eve had departed from the instruction of God (through their fear) and chose their own way by eating of the *Tree of the Knowledge of Good and Evil*, the result was an immediate and subsequent *increase* in fear. They hid from God, as they became gravely afraid.

> *"And they heard the sound of YHWH God walking in the garden in the cool of the day, and Adam and his wife **hid themselves** from the presence of YHWH God among the trees of the garden. Then YHWH God called to Adam and said to him, 'Where are you?' So he said, 'I heard Your voice in the garden, and **I was afraid** because I was naked; and I **hid** myself.'"* (Gen. 3:8-10)

Adam and Eve were unwilling to face up to the Creator, and tried to hide themselves instead. Ever since, a similar experience of intense fear has become a primary plague of humanity. In line with this, the basic human reaction to the sharp discomfort of fear has been to grasp after pseudo-safety by means of seeking human rulers to take the reins, and fight our battles on our behalf.

However, as we know, and as history has told us, *human kingship* does not solve our human predicament. To the contrary, in most cases, tyranny reigns, and pain of all kinds is rampant. This means that we need to be willing to take another look at reality. We need to rethink our beliefs about what 'works,' chiefly because what humans have been doing now for millennia does *not* work. This is evidenced by the multiplicity of wars, injustices, and injurious forms of oppression that we have seen over the years.

We need to somehow learn to be different. But how?

Certainly, there is nothing wrong with human *leadership*, when exercised by healthy, humble, and wise individuals. As we have been discussing, leadership is our God-given, human responsibility. Yet, He has not asked us to lead alone without Him.

Herein lies the secret: when God is directing human affairs, we will all be connected with the perfect leadership role for which we are each individually fitted. In His infinite love and wisdom, it will also be the role that brings us, and others around us, the most joy. What we're essentially seeing is the great need for us to tune into the fact that our Creator is the *sole* King over all of humanity. He is our Leader and our Guide, and it is to Him that we can look for direct instruction.

He is the One in Whom we can place all of our trust: for *direction*, *love*, and *care*. Accordingly, we can take what we are given from His hand, and His guidance, and then reflect

it in our own special leadership position. As long as we
carry this out with a confident, yet humble, diligence in our
hearts we will be in harmony with other people. Together in
this way, we will lovingly rule over the rest of the plant and
animal kingdoms: the life forms which were always
intended to be in our charge. If we pursue this amazing
calling, we will each become a gorgeous gift to the world in
our own unique way.

> *"Yours, O YHWH, is the greatness and the power and the glory
> and the victory and the majesty, indeed everything that is in the
> heavens and the earth; Yours is the dominion, O YHWH, and You
> exalt Yourself as Head over all."* (1 Chr. 29:11)

> *"Trust in YHWH with all your heart, and lean not on your own
> understanding; in all your ways acknowledge Him, and He shall
> direct your paths. Do not be wise in your own eyes; fear
> YHWH and depart from evil. It will be health to your flesh, and
> strength to your bones."*
> (Pro. 3:5-8)

It is important to be aware that the common competitive
mindset that we are familiar with in Western culture has
caused us to feel that if someone else wins then, by necessity,
we must therefore lose (or vice versa). Yet, in truth, it
doesn't have to be this way. If we tune into our purpose, we
will find that it is truly unique; this also signifies that we
have no one else to compete against, other than challenging
the *self* to greater levels of mastery and excellence. By this
means, we will have so much to offer and to give to the
world. This ultimately creates the splendid situation
wherein all of us will benefit by the lives, efforts, and
successes of every other person, while we concurrently
continue to pursue greatness in our individual life-calling.

There is an important difference between true human *leadership* according to God's design, and the human-derived *kingdoms of men*. Under human kingship, we give up our true humanity. We give up our responsibility and capacity for leadership to someone else. Consequently, that *someone else* walks away from their true life purpose (as well as their true gifts) in order to rule over other people instead. Since being disconnected from our potential and purpose in life breeds a situation that can never bring true happiness, this also may be the very reason that, historically, various forms of addiction have been rampant among kings, emperors, and the elite of the world.

> *"The trees once went forth to anoint a king over them.*
> *And they said to the olive tree,*
> *'Reign over us!'*
> *But the olive tree said to them,*
> *'Should I cease giving my oil,*
> *With which God and men are honored,*
> *And go to sway over trees?'"*
> (Jud. 9:8-9)

God's original intention with humanity is one of harmony, closeness to Him, and unity. When we tune into His original design for us, and connect with the leadership roles He is calling us to, we will be drawing closer to that beautiful day when all the earth will be filled with glorious perfection. Throughout our lives, there will be various roles of leadership that we are called to: according to life circumstances, and our own personal growth. We'll learn to flow with, and connect with our God, being flexible while trusting in Him. In addition, we will find gorgeous harmony with one another and all other life on the earth.

We will have our hearts opened to see the incredible beauty of *shalom* into eternity.

> *"Commit your way to YHWH, trust also in Him. Delight yourself also in YHWH, and He shall give you the desires of your heart."* (Psa. 37:5,4)

> *"YHWH sits as King forever. YHWH will give strength to His people; YHWH will bless His people with shalom."*
> (Psa. 29:10-11)

6

A Craving for Human Kingship

Curiously enough, throughout history humans have been plagued by the spiritual turmoil caused by an intense personal conflict between the programmed self, and our true essence. This has served to produce a rather perplexing paradox in terms of our spiritual experience. The human enigma can be easily observed when we consider the fact that human-beings hate to be controlled, and yet, at the same time they crave the life of a slave. How can this be? For the most part, servitude has simply become our comfort zone, as we have progressively distanced ourselves from the higher, healthier *Eden* dynamic. It's just what we've always known as we have allowed our social-selves to adapt to a divergent reality, and a perverse order of things.

"We remember the fish which we used to eat free in Egypt, the cucumbers and the melons and the leeks and the onions and the garlic." (Num. 11:5)

Being controlled, in many ways, is actually quite *easy*. It may not be easy on our spirit, nor produce happiness, and it certainly does not help us to reach our potential as human beings. Nonetheless, at the same time, the sheer predictability of a controlled environment and a familiar life breeds a feeling of complacency in knowing what to expect, even when that expectation is far from the ideals of what we truly desire, deep down inside our hearts.

Stepping outside of the confines of the world's controls means that we will have to live courageously, and ultimately face our fears. This is because, in reality, we actually have nothing to fear if we are aligning ourselves with the Creator in a spirit of trust. One of the hidden truths that we positively need to understand in this quest, however, is the way in which the emotional reaction of fear has been conditioned into us in a variety of ways, and from an early age. By means of public education, a variety of media, and the destabilized mentality of the people around us, we are taught to be afraid of being different; we are taught to believe that human integrity lies in becoming 'contributing citizens of society,' and in the collective participation of propping up the system *as it is*. All the while, creativity, wonder, and uniqueness are pushed to the side.

Early in their history, the nation of Israel asked for a human king. God had previously anticipated this, as we see in the early writings of Moses (Deu. 17:14). God's anticipation is not surprising, of course, as He is by no means confined by time in His infinite foreknowledge. Yet, based on the common tendencies of humanity since the time of Adam and Eve, it is possible that any mindful person may have been able to predict that eventually Israel would want a king, as long as they continued living below their potential. As it happened, that's precisely how things played out. This is shown to us in the record of the prophet Samuel (the last of the judges) where the people begin to ask for a king: *like the other nations* that surrounded them.

> *"Then all the elders of Israel gathered together and came to Samuel at Ramah, and said to him, 'Look, you are old, and your sons do not walk in your ways.* **Now make us a king to judge us like all the nations.**'" (1 Sam. 8:4-5)

It is important to point out that this tendency to look for a human king is closely connected to the events that we see playing out with Adam and Eve in the garden.

In the Genesis account we see that Eve, in her fear, distrust and disconnection, ends up looking to the serpent as a source of authority and mediatorship, rather than the Creator. In essence, she *exalted* the serpent by following *his instructions*. Ironically, even though she was pursuing her own personal authority, in line with her belief in the serpent's promise that she would be "like God" if she ate: in actuality, by giving in to the serpent's counsel, she ultimately bowed herself down to a base creature. In this she decidedly *surrendered* the personal authority that was already hers by Divine appointment, from the beginning. In effect, she allowed the serpent to direct her paths for her. Even more, as we know, along with Adam she had even been given authority over the *entirety* of the creation. She lost sight of this authority, however, and in a tragic departure from her design: she surrendered it at the feet of the serpent. These details provide an invaluable education for us, helping us to recognize the distorted mindset that we have inherited (in order that we may ultimately find transcendence, once and for all).

The Fallen in the Earth

As we become more intimate with the overall, genuine message of the Hebrew Scriptures, we discover that the events in the garden become a precursor for the unfolding of world events. By the beginning of Genesis chapter six, we see that *rulers of men* were rising up in the earth, and becoming princes over the people.

Let me first underline the point that this chapter is full of somewhat puzzling details, yet we will nevertheless find that a greater contextual picture will help demystify some of its more peculiar-seeming aspects. So let's take a closer look.

Many suppositions have certainly been made about this section of Scripture in Genesis, primarily because of the term, "*The Sons of God*." Once again, we will set aside preconceived ideas, as we prayerfully endeavor to see the narrative afresh.

Genesis 6:1-6

"Now it came to pass, when men began to multiply on the face of the earth, and daughters were born to them, that the sons of God

saw the daughters of men, that they were beautiful; and they took wives for themselves of all whom they chose.

And YHWH said, 'My Spirit shall not strive with man forever, for he is indeed flesh; yet his days shall be one hundred and twenty years.'

There were giants on the earth in those days, and also afterward, when the sons of God came in to the daughters of men and they bore children to them. Those were the mighty men who were of old, men of renown.

Then YHWH saw that the wickedness of man was great in the earth, and that every intent of the thoughts of his heart was only evil continually. And YHWH was sorry that He had made man on the earth, and He was grieved in His heart."

_ _

When considering the meaning of the above passage, most people miss the fact that we are reading a narrative dealing with the grievous outcome of power having been heaped upon men (who have essentially become dictatorial rulers over multitudes). Because human-beings had forgotten who they were, as the original leaders upon the earth, they instead bowed themselves to other created beings.

This same mentality is the reason for all forms of idolatry (visible gods & mediators), as well as the corruption behind the *kingdoms of men* in its entirety. No matter which organized, false belief-system we look at, they are all based upon a disconnection from the Creator, and a man-made attempt to calm, or pacify, the distress of fear. Historically, some civilizations have taken this to such an extreme, so as to develop imaginations that are *"only evil continually,"* as we see in the record leading up to the Genesis flood.

So let's look at the passage at the beginning of Genesis six, in detail, as we seek to understand what it's really getting at. To do so, we will need to delve into the original Hebrew for a number of the words we find in this passage, in order to gain a richer understanding.

In brief, we come across the following somewhat mysterious words being mentioned (as commonly seen in English translations):

- *"sons of God"*
- *"giants"*
- *"mighty men"*
- *"men of renown"*

It doesn't take much of a stretch of the imagination to observe how these titles, even in their basic English translations, point to the theme of human kingship in the earth. What we discover is that, even in humankind's ancient history, the world was not particularly different in its societal structure then – than what it has been ever since. We have just seen varying flavors, forms, and degrees of authoritarian rule, in diverse civilizations. Even today, though we have many governments that we would classify as *"democratic,"* we still have a real situation in which the world's elite (or those who hold most of the world's wealth) hold the cards of command. *"He who has the most gold makes the rules,"* so to speak.

Getting back to Genesis six, what becomes immediately evident from this passage is that at this time in the earth's history, there was a sharp distinction between two groups of people. The two recorded groups are: "*men*" and "*the sons of God.*" The question then becomes, *where did this distinction come from?* Was it a *God-made* or a *man-made* distinction?

It's valuable to note that this is the first appearance of the term "*sons of God*" in the Biblical record. We neither have any evidence that this particular class of people, in Genesis 6, were so named by Divine intention, nor that they were the original people of God. In other words, this passage does *not* indicate that these "*Sons of God*" actually *were* the sons of the True Creator, and it also doesn't specify that this group was granted its title by the Creator. In actuality, it appears as though this grouping may have been a *man-made* class of people, referred to in their day as "*The Sons of God*," respectively. Namely, *The Sons of God* was a human-ordained, sovereign title, rather than a reference to a God-ordained, Godly community.

Perhaps this interpretation may not yet seem plausible to you as the reader, but keep in mind that we have yet to consider the evidence. At this point, I ask only for an open mind in considering these things. We'll start by looking more at the original Hebrew, in order to determine the primary meanings. For ease of reviewing these details, I have included the Hebrew study of this passage in a table, as follows. I encourage the reader to carefully read through the table in its entirety, for the sake of clarity and proper understanding in relation to the evidence presented.

Genesis 6:1-4 Study Notes

<u>**Verses 1-2**</u> "Now it came to pass, when <u>men</u> began to multiply on the face of the earth, and daughters were born to them, that the <u>sons of God</u> saw the daughters of <u>men</u>, that they were <u>beautiful</u>; and they took wives for themselves of all whom they chose."	Here we see that we have moved along in the history of humankind – and within the span of time from the time of Adam and Eve to this period, events have occurred that led to the existence of two separate groups of people – 1) "men" (who bring forth beautiful daughters) and 2) "The Sons of God."
	The Hebrew word for "God" in this verse, is not the singular "*El*," but the plural "*Elohim*" – meaning "*mighties*." This is a word that has a broad application in the Hebrew, commonly used of the True Creator, as well as false 'gods' or false 'mighties.' Thus, we find here the "*Sons of Elohim*" or "*Mighties*."
	The Hebrew word for "beautiful" in reference to the daughters of men is actually "*towb*" – meaning "*good*." It is the exact same Hebrew word that is used in relation to the original design of the creative works of God's hand: the things that were "good" in the sight of God. As we see here, at least in the eyes of these "Sons of Elohim" – these *daughters of men* were seen as "good."
	It appears, based on the details given here, that the "Sons of God" group did as they pleased – and that whichever women they thought were *good* and wanted to have as a wife – they simply took without any barrier or restriction. This certainly points to the idea that this was a class of people who were somehow able to extract from the rest of humanity whatever they pleased (See 1 Sam. 8:10-18). It also parallels what we have seen down through history: that within the ruling classes (kings in particular), the men commonly had a large number of wives.

Verses 3-4 "And YHWH said, 'My Spirit shall not strive with man forever, for he is indeed flesh; yet his days shall be one hundred and twenty years.' There were <u>giants</u> on the earth in those days, and also afterward, when the sons of God came in to the daughters of men and they bore <u>children</u> to them. Those were the <u>mighty men</u> who were of old, <u>men</u> of <u>renown</u>."	The Hebrew word for "giants" is *Něphiyl*. It is only used three times in the entirety of the Hebrew Scriptures. It is also notably used of the "sons of Anak" who were present in the land of Canaan at the time of the Exodus. Its meaning is made clear when we look at the original root word from which it comes: *"naphal"* – which means *"to fall."*
	The Hebrew word for "children" is *"hām."* It generally means *"the same."* In other words, the *Sons of God* married the *daughters of men*, and their wives bore *the same* to them.
	The single Hebrew word translated as "mighty men" is *"gibbowr."* It means 'powerful,' 'strong,' or 'those who prevail.' It is often used of powerful, tyrannical warrior peoples who walk contrary to the Creator in their own strength; though the word can also be used in a positive sense as well.
	The Hebrew word for "men," in the context of *"men of renown"* is *"enowsh."* It is the word that refers to men in their mortality, or their mortal state. This is interesting, as it negates a commonly understood concept that these *mighty men of renown* were some kind of supernatural race. The Scriptures don't seem to be supporting this with the usage of the Hebrew word *enowsh,* in this context. It is also interesting to note that this word comes from a Hebrew root word: *"anash,"* which means to be weak, ill, sick or frail – often translated as "incurable."
	The Hebrew word for "renown" is *"shem."* It is the word that commonly and generally refers to a *"name."* This is the Hebrew word that is used in the context of both the names of men, as well as the name of God.

For our purposes here, one of the most significant discoveries in our Hebrew study is the understanding that the Hebrew word for *giants* actually means "*fallen.*" When looking more closely at the Hebrew itself, a more appropriate translation of Gen. 6:4 would be:

> "The **_fallen_** were in the earth in those days, and also, after that when the sons of God came into the daughters of men, and they bore to them the same, those were the mighty men who were of old, men of renown."

By reading carefully in the Hebrew, we observe that those who were called "*the fallen*" were not necessarily the same group as the "*Sons of God*" or the "*mighty men.*" This being the case, it becomes clear that there is actually a chronological progression in the narrative of this passage. Let's briefly observe this pattern:

1. "*The fallen*" among humanity appear in the earth.

2. The record goes on to specify that "*also, after that*" – the *Sons of God* have children with the daughters of men.

3. This eventually results in the appearance of the "*mighty men*" who were considered "*men of renown.*"

The progression can be highlighted as follows (from Gen. 6:4):

> "*There were the fallen on the earth in those days*" → "*and also afterward*" → "*when the sons of God came in to the daughters of men and they bore the same to them,*" → "*those were the mighty men who were of old, men of renown.*"

In other words, a *fallen people's* presence in the earth became a prime breeding ground for the advancement of a ruling class of "*mighty men.*" It is probable that the description of "*the fallen*" is referring to the masses of people who had become *fallen* in the sense that they were disconnected from who they were originally created to be, as leaders in the earth.

The argument here, then, is that human disconnection from our exalted potential for leadership is what gave rise to the tyrannical regime that ruled over the rest of humanity. This is also the reason that the earth became filled with violence. Doubtlessly, great evils were done at the hands of this ruling class, and the great oppressiveness of this man-made system caused the breakdown of society, at every level imaginable. And it is no mystery that the degeneration of civilization itself ultimately leads to the outward reality of violence among peoples who are no longer in touch with their ability to rise above unnecessary conflict.

Interestingly, the Hebrew root word for "*the fallen*" appears back in Genesis chapter four, within the narrative we were previously considering (Heb. "*naphal*").

> "*And YHWH respected Abel and his offering, but He did not respect Cain and his offering. And Cain was very angry, and his countenance **fell**. So YHWH said to Cain, 'Why are you angry? And why has your countenance **fallen**?'*" (Gen. 4:4-6)

When Cain's offering was not respected, instead of reflecting on "*why*," we see that he does not utilize his capacity for higher consciousness. Instead he allows automatic, reactive anger to dominate. He surrenders himself to the anger that wells up inside of him, and enters into a state wherein he is *"fallen"* in his person. He becomes *ruled over* by the reactionary, base emotions which were to bring about destructive evil into his midst. In Cain's life, this meant a disturbance so severe, that he even becomes a murderer within the circle of his own family.

When we consider the account in Genesis chapter four within the same context as the events in chapter six, it is fascinating to discover a number of important parallels. These parallels are outlined in the following table:

Cain *(Genesis Four)*	**Multiplying Men** *(Genesis Six)*
Narrative opens with reference to Adam and Eve *multiplying*. Eve gives birth to Cain and Abel.	Narrative opens with reference to *men multiplying on the earth*. Note that the Hebrew word here for "men" is also "Adam."
Cain strives with God by bucking against God's order and Leadership. He is not interested in why God did not accept his offering. He wants to do things his way.	We see the following statement in Gen. 6:3: *"And YHWH said, 'My Spirit shall not <u>strive</u> with man forever.'"* This is a clear indication that humanity, in general, was bucking against His Leadership and order.
After God does not accept Cain's offering, the record specifies that Cain's countenance became *fallen*.	The record specifies that *"there was the fallen on the earth in those days."* The Hebrew word for *"the fallen"* is related to the same Hebrew word that is found in Gen. 4, in reference to Cain's fallen countenance.

Cain	Multiplying Men
After Cain *falls* in his person, he allows base, reactive, distorted thinking to rule over him.	After the *fallen* collective of people appear in the earth, they collectively allow a base, reactive, distorted dynasty to rule over them.
The reactive mind so overwhelms Cain, that he acts out in violence and murders his brother.	The base-minded, ruling regime so overwhelms the masses of humanity (doing whatever they pleased) that the entire earth becomes filled with violence.
We see God's abiding love and mercy being spoken of, as He decides that Cain should still live, and He therefore places a mark of protection over him. (Gen. 4:13-15).	We see God's abiding love and mercy being spoken of, as He decides to preserve humanity through Noah: *"But Noah found grace in the eyes of YHWH."*

Just as Genesis chapter four deals with an *individual* who becomes fallen from the true potential that was placed within him, Genesis chapter six likewise deals with an entire *society* that becomes fallen in their *collective* consciousness. In both cases, severe violence ensues.

In Genesis chapter six, we see that *"the fallen"* have come to be on the earth. We recognize in this appearance, a collective of people who live entirely according to a baseline of debased fear, rather than exalted trust. This is confirmed by the phrase: *"Then YHWH saw that the wickedness of man was great in the earth, and that every intent of the thoughts of his heart was only evil continually."*

So we see a society removed from their connection to the Creator, altogether forgetting who they really are. The cultural norm, then, became that of a serpentine reactivity, and a degraded level of thinking, instead of the exalted consciousness that God had gifted humanity with from the very beginning.

Moving on, as indicated in the above table, the Hebrew word for "*children*" in this passage is "*hām*" which actually means "*the same.*" This establishes the following translation:

> "*There were fallen on the earth in those days, and also afterward, when the sons of God came in to the daughters of men and they bore **the same** to them.*" (Gen. 6:4)

In other words, the *daughters of men* gave birth to children who were "*the same*" as their predecessors *The Sons of God*. What is being illustrated here is the concept of a dynasty: with a sequence of rulers all arising from the same family lineage. Or, to put it another way, royalty is bringing forth more royalty. The throne is passed down through *the same* family line, and each ruler would only continue to manifest *the same* character as their fathers.

This is further evidenced with the next Scriptural phrase: "*Those were the mighty men who were of old, men of a name.*" By extension, the dynasty of *The Sons of God* also became known as *the mighty* upon the earth. These were the sovereign ones – the ones who had become "*men of a name,*" and who were ultimately the *mighty* upon the earth. This hierarchical order then becomes a very powerful precedent for the unfolding of human history, thereafter.

The Mighty Hunter

Though the violent generation found in Genesis chapter six finds its end in the Biblical flood, it is not long before multitudes of people again begin organizing themselves in similar fashion. In a cyclical manner, the same theme picks up again in Genesis chapter ten, with the notorious story of Nimrod. Let's take a closer look at this narrative.

Incorporating the same mentality as those who lived before the flood, the descendants of Noah fell right back into their inherited tendency to seek deliverance, salvation, and leadership at the hands of another human being.

In his generation, Nimrod, the infamous founder of Babel, apparently saw a grand opportunity to pursue a position of power over the people. Considering the fact that people had learned to find safety and comfort in a human ruler, it would be easy to deceivingly take advantage of this, for any individual inclined to do so.

Once again, although we do not have a lot of details about Nimrod, the few details we do have are of great value, and carry significant meaning.

We find the following passage in Genesis chapter 10:

> *"Cush begot **Nimrod; he began to be a mighty one on the earth. He was a mighty hunter before YHWH; therefore it is said, "Like Nimrod the mighty hunter before YHWH."** And the beginning of his **kingdom** was Babel, Erech, Accad, and Calneh, in the land of Shinar. From that land he went to Assyria and built Nineveh, Rehoboth Ir, Calah, and Resen between Nineveh and Calah (that is the principal city)."* (Gen. 10:8-12)

There are many keys for us to consider in this short passage.

First of all, note that the passage is very clear in establishing the fact that Nimrod is setting himself up as king. We find the phrase *"the beginning of his kingdom,"* indicating that he becomes the king of a large population, extending over multiple cities.

It is interesting to note, however, that even though Nimrod was a king, the record is drawing our attention primarily to his role as a *"mighty hunter."* Just what are we to discern from this? Here are a few suggestions:

- A hunter is one who exerts power over the animal kingdom. As we have been discussing at length, when human beings capitulate to a reactive, base mindset, they begin to operate in similar fashion to inferior animals (rather than the exalted creature that we are designed to be). It can be easily surmised that Nimrod had learned to control the populace by means of taking advantage of the fears of his subjects. Thus, as a *"mighty hunter,"* his political and religious exploits would achieve a powerful mastery over a population of retrograde, highly-willing subjects.
- A hunter is also one who is skilled with weaponry. It is likely that Nimrod was looked to for protection, deliverance, and salvation; by a fearful collective, desperate to find a semblance of safety. After all, he was their mighty hunter.
- The repetition of the word *"mighty"* in this passage points us back to Genesis chapter six. It is the very same Hebrew word (*gibbowr*) used in relation to the

"*mighty ones*" who had risen up before the flood. Here it is emphasized through its repetition three times: in direct reference to Nimrod. This repeated usage of "*gibbowr*" also confirms that, at this time, society was looking to Nimrod as a source of external might and safety, rather than realizing their own access to their true "Mighty One," the "El" of Israel.[7]

We see that Nimrod had both an illustrious name, as well as an influential reputation in His day. It would appear that he became a source of admiration, and a measuring stick for people to look up to. We see this phrase appearing in verse nine:

"Therefore it is said,
'Even as Nimrod,
The Mighty Hunter Before YHWH.'"

Note: The phrase "*before YHWH*" is
significant in the Hebrew.
In Hebrew, "*before*" is "*paniym*" –
meaning "*in the face of.*"

In other words, people were habitually speaking among themselves in the vein of "*Even as Nimrod, the mighty hunter before YHWH.*" He was their king, after all, and was infamously known in this manner. In this way, we see that "*The Mighty Hunter in the Face of YHWH*" was a man-made title assigned to Nimrod, the king (just as the term "*The Sons of God*" was being used in Genesis chapter 6). So with that being the case, then, what did this actually mean to them, on a spiritual level? How was he a mighty hunter *in God's face* according to the understanding of the people?

It is evident that, according to the details we have been given, Nimrod had been set up as a false *representative of God* among the people. People perceived that when they looked at this mighty king Nimrod, they were basically seeing the Divine Face of God. With gross distortion, they regarded him as a glorious physical manifestation of Divinity. To the people, he was the mighty hunter who had subdued the earth under his feet. He was their mighty king, believed to be the singular expression of the Creator Himself. In other words, Nimrod had created a grand, misguided religious system, with a so-called "*Divine King*" at its helm.

On the contrary, the fact that Nimrod was "*in God's face*" would have meant something quite different to the Creator. It is interesting that the word "*paniym*" (Hebrew for "face") comes from a Hebrew root word meaning "*to turn*." This is because we know that Nimrod, and the activities that he was partaking in, were in direct opposition to God. In other words, these activities associated with Nimrod and his kingdom were *a turning away* from the Creator's established paradigm of leadership.

In line with all that we have been looking at in Genesis thus far, it seems quite probable that this passage concerning Nimrod is pointing to the following:

- That Nimrod became a great ruler upon the earth, standing in the place of God. He positioned himself in *YHWH's face*, in the breach between God and men, as a *false representative*. Nimrod built numerous cities upon the earth as we see in Genesis chapter 10, all of which he likely ruled over.

- That Nimrod's leadership blocked the true God from view. He stood "*in His face*" in the hearts of the people. In this way, he became a stumbling block to the people – specifically, by obstructing their ability to connect with their Creator.

- That Nimrod was a man who did not look towards God for Divine Leadership, but *turned away* from God and *turned towards* the people – facing towards them as a so-called Divine leader. He arrogantly positioned himself as if he was exalted above the people, in the place of God.

The events that follow in Babel comprise one of the most famous Bible stories of all time: the building of the "*Tower of Babel.*" We are not definitely told whether these events were specifically contemporary with the time of Nimrod, or afterwards under a form of government set up by Nimrod in the cities he founded. It is certainly possible, however, that these events did happen under Nimrod's direct leadership. Regardless of the timing, the details concerning this event give further confirmation for the truths that we have already been uncovering.

The Biblical details concerning the building of the *Tower of Babel* are as follows:

Genesis 11:1-9

*"Now **the whole earth** had one language and one speech. And it came to pass, as they journeyed from the east, that they found a plain in the land of Shinar, and they dwelt there.*

Then they said to one another, 'Come, let us make bricks and bake them thoroughly.' They had brick for stone, and they had asphalt for mortar.

*And they said, '**Come, let us build ourselves a city, and a tower whose top is in the heavens; let us make a name for ourselves, lest we be scattered abroad over the face of the whole earth**.'*

But YHWH came down to see the city and the tower which the sons of men had built. And YHWH said, 'Indeed the people are one and they all have one language, and this is what they begin to do; now nothing that they propose to do will be withheld from them.

Come, let Us go down and there confuse their language, that they may not understand one another's speech.' So YHWH scattered them abroad from there over the face of all the earth, and they ceased building the city.

***Therefore its name is called Babel**, because there YHWH confused the language of all the earth; and from there YHWH scattered them abroad over the face of all the earth."*

These are interesting events, indeed, particularly since there are so many parallels with what we have been looking at. Once again, we primarily see the people seeking an *external manifestation* of that which they already held in the core of their person – which is the essence of Divine connection.

It is obvious that a major motivation for the building of the tower of Babel is *fear*. This is evident by the conferred reasoning of, "*lest we be scattered abroad over the face of the whole earth.*"

Ultimately, the people are afraid of finding themselves alone, and they seek to find connection via proximity with other people, in the context of noisy city life. They begin building a city and a tower to the heavens, with the intention of connecting with God, and maintaining connection with each other. This was all executed outside of the higher awareness: that authentic connection is that which is found inwardly. No matter how many ritualistic variations of spirituality we invent ourselves, if connection is being sought in a purely external manner, it will continue to be lost on us. Simply put, genuine connection will never come from an external construct of men.

We also find in this narrative the recognizable concept that the perceived fears of humanity would ultimately manifest into an experienced reality (this is true whether just in an individual, or collectively, in a social community). Specifically, they are afraid of being scattered abroad, and yet it's the very thing that ends up happening. We can see that their fear becomes a catalyst for their actions, and their actions lead to the very thing that they were afraid would happen. That is, their fear-based consciousness *becomes* their reality.

Another continuing theme that we find interwoven into this chapter, is that, yet again there is a group of people seeking to *make a name for themselves*. This is the very same concept that was presented in Genesis chapter six, referring to the "*men of a name*," who were the elite ruling class prior to the flood.

> "And **_they_ said**, "Come, let us build ourselves a city, and a tower whose top is in the heavens; let us make ***a name for ourselves***..."
> (Gen. 11:4)

It is certainly plausible that the "*they*" who spoke in Genesis chapter eleven is referring to Babel's ruling class, who were intending to *make a name for themselves* and gain notoriety among the people. In that case, the apprehension around people being spread abroad would have been induced by the fear that they would lose the opportunity to continue to control the multitudes of people then on the earth. Thus, they were seeking dictatorial rule, over as large a population as possible within their grand city.

Since the Creator knew where all these efforts would lead, in this instance, He decides to intervene. He confuses their language – creating a wide variety of 'tongues' and scatters the people throughout the earth. Consequently, it was because of this very event that the city became known as "*Babel*" – meaning "*confusion*." And so, Babel becomes a fitting symbol for the confusion of false religions, and the distorted systems of men: each fueled by human fear, and glued together with human confusion.

Yet, this is not where the story of humanity ends, as we are blessed to see. We're being led on an extraordinary journey here, and we're being taken through a momentous process of transformation.

With this renewed understanding of our history, it's time for us to find within ourselves the motivation to become the leaders we were always meant to be.

Moving Forward

Whenever we encounter various forms of physical illness, we know that it is important for us to uncover the root cause of the malady, in order to fully pursue healing. We need to gain knowledge, insight, and understanding with regards to the causative factors, as well as the healing elements, that are relevant to any human health crisis. Similarly, on a global level, generations of humanity have been painfully experiencing a crisis of *disconnection*, which ultimately leads to sickness, and eventually to death. At this stage in the game, to varying degrees, we are all disconnected from the Divine, from our true self, and from each other.

Fear, as we are demonstrating through the pages of this book, is the primary cause of this disconnection. This is why the symptoms of this collective malady include the human tendency to cling to false forms of comfort and safety. The common craving for a human king and the adherence to man-made false religion is a signal that we need to find true healing, and lasting transformation.

Healing will come when we embark on a journey of reconnection, while we concurrently learn to dwell in trust. The ancient stories recorded in early Genesis are a marvelous gift, helping us to develop the skill of recognizing human malady for what it is: for the very reason of ascending to something better. This exalted recognition will be the key of our ability to make that ascension, without having to fall back on the false securities that fear blinds us with.

We have been conditioned to look to other authorities, other kings, other gods, and other external religions; all of these outward sources *appear* to satiate our spiritual thirsts and cravings while we desperately grasp at some kind of direction. Yet, none of these can ever genuinely fulfill us. They are never able to remove our fears, and they can never bring lasting peace. In fact, external authorities will often *utilize* our fears in order to promote unwavering allegiance, "*or else*."

Throughout history, people have been seeking human lordship, deliverance and direction, by means of human sovereignty, and religious masters. In Western Civilization, in our day, this propensity can also be seen when we put our democratic leaders, academic authorities, media experts, or religious ministers on a pedestal, and place a fundamental trust in them which – almost exclusively – is ill-suited to their actual abilities as a human being. For, despite all the vast knowledge that fills the world, all of this information has yet to bring a solution to a world that is very much still full of turmoil, pain, and fear. And try as we might to drown out our sharp pain by means of distracting ourselves with entertainment, addictions, and social noise, our problems will never be solved by these means. We will never see healing until we realize who we truly are; what we have been created for; Who God is; and what He wants us to be doing, according to His ways and design.

These realizations are an absolute *must*, and the greatest blessing is that He has promised us that this is certain to be our future. There will one day be a global return to the Garden, and an extensive awareness of all that is real, true and Divine. One day we will finally awake to our truest potential in our connection with God, ourselves, and with each other. We will become a true, collective *Prince with Our God*.

I believe that many are beginning to wake up to this, even now.

7

Prince With El

What if we have forgotten who we are?

What if, in fact, this forgotten truth goes all the way back to our very beginnings?

These are primary questions that have been underlying all that we have been considering thus far. For those of us who believe in the significance of the Hebrew Bible, most of us will intrinsically realize that *all of us* have forgotten our original, God-given heritage, at least in some way or another.

As we saw in our opening pages, Adam and Eve had been given a glorious heritage upon their entry into life. They were marvelously blessed to be made after the *image* and *likeness* of the Eternal God Who created them. They were also called to have *dominion* over the rest of the creation. They were called to rule together as loving leaders and perfect ambassadors of the love and kindness of their Heavenly Father - as He helped them take care of all of the other elements of life that He had made. He also instructed them to "*guard*" and to "*serve*" the magnificent garden that He had given them to live in: to be servant-guardians over the perfect, harmonious work of their God.

In other words, they were made to be *co-leaders* in the context of their personal relationship with the *Divine King of the Universe*.

Humanity was created for the very purpose of leadership. We were made *to rule*. Yet, it is imperative to note that God's version of *rulership* is far different than what societies have historically known. For millennia, we have become familiar with the existence of human kings, emperors, authorities and rulers. Amazingly, at the very same time, most of humanity has been entirely disconnected from the animals that populate the globe. It is strange to consider that, on one hand, God had originally intended for us to be loving and attentive leaders over all animal life. Yet, for generations we've had so little interaction with the animals that populate our planet, to the point that we are generally clueless about them. The original order of things that God had declared to be "*very good*" is, in effect, poles apart from the world that we have known.

It is also a rare thing, for that matter, for humans to even recognize the design of their own person - let alone interact with it in any meaningful kind of way. With improper understanding concerning the blue-print of our human make-up, then, we have also been rendered inadvertently unaware of how to govern the *self*. Instead, we have been allowing ourselves to be ruled-over, rather than taking the wheel and wisely steering our own person.

In our quest to healthfully respond to our individual and collective calling, we have to shift our thinking and embrace the wisdom concerning our own human-animal elements. We need to understand how our brain and body both operate, in order to pioneer and captain the physical self for success. To be truly effective in this manner, it is integral that we attentively perceive our true nature and the original blueprint of our design. We need to know that our *true self* is the element of our consciousness that is able to connect with the Divine Consciousness, while rising above all the superfluous thoughts that show up in our awareness. In this fashion, we need to know that we are not the thoughts that appear in our consciousness, but rather we are *the being* that can observe the thoughts, and see them for what they are. Ultimately, we need to know ourselves according to the gift of our amazing potential and our ability to soar to great Spiritual heights.

Furthermore, we all need to appreciate the importance of gaining true insight with regards to ourselves, and the other elements of the creation, in order to be the effective leaders we were born to be. Lovingly and patiently, our God is calling us to turn away from the broken system of things that we have accepted for so long.

He is calling us back to our beginning, so that we can come to recognize *who we really are*.

Who is Israel?

Raising this simple question, *"Who is Israel?"* is likely to invoke strong emotions of various kinds for many Biblically-minded individuals, depending on their particular theological background. I'd like to assure you that I'm not here to enter into the controversies surrounding this question. What I do invite, however, is the willingness to let go of our preconceived ideas as part of our overall quest to raise our understanding to meet the elevated consciousness of the infinite Creator. Accordingly, I encourage you to delve into this study with joy, peace, and excited anticipation of the gorgeous truths that our God is willing to reveal to us, in the context of our enquiry.

With that in mind, *"Who is Israel?"*

There is a stunning and rarely understood truth concerning the true essence of the Biblical *Israel*. Apart from anything else, Israel was to be a nation of *transcendence*. From the outset of its inception, it was to be a conscious collective that would rise above the base, egoic thinking that – up until that point – had become the norm of humanity.

If we are to understand the true nature of the Israel of the Bible, we need to view these things from the exalted perspective of the Divine Consciousness. We cannot analyze its designs from human-derived concepts: whether social, political or even religious, for that matter. Instead, we need to comprehend that the essence of *Israel* is in perfect harmony with the entire message of the Hebrew Bible itself, including the insights available to us in the earlier Biblical narrative of Genesis.

As we see in the Biblical history concerning the failings of 'national' Israel, it can be deduced that to be *physically* part of the lineage of Jacob was simply not enough in order to manifest the grand, holistic purpose of God: that the rest of the planet would be greatly blessed, and healed, through this collective of people. Nonetheless, it is the premise of this book that the Divine is *not finished* with the physical lineage of Jacob, and that He is *dynamically* faithful to fulfill His ancient promises. In like manner, He is also not finished with the rest of humanity's destiny to fulfill His promises of global healing and prosperity. The true essence of Israel, therefore, is to be a *witness* to the rest of humanity, so that everyone may finally be enlightened to their true nature, and reconnected to their true potential.

> *"But now, thus says YHWH, who created you, **O Jacob**, and He who formed you, **O Israel**: 'Fear not, for I have redeemed you; I have called you by your name; you are Mine'… **'You are My witnesses**,' says YHWH, 'And My servant whom I have chosen, that you may know and believe Me, and understand that I am He. Before Me there was no God formed, nor shall there be after Me.'"*
> (Isa. 43:1,10)

In a very real sense, the nation of Israel was brought into being in order to demonstrate the responsibility and the tremendous, purposeful potential of *every true human being*. This is the way in which the nation of Israel was to become Yah's great *witness* upon the earth. True Israel was to demonstrate His purpose for humanity from the beginning, so that we may understand Who the Creator is, come to know Him, and discover what has always been in His heart to do.

In other words, "*Israel*" is the inherited name of every person who has learned to transcend the base, reactive thinking we were born into, and it is the true term for the individual who has aspired to seek transformation into his or her *true self*, as we were originally designed to be.

> *"This one will say, 'I am YHWH's; another will call himself by the name of Jacob; still another will write on his hand, 'YHWH's,' and name himself by the name of Israel.'"* (Isa. 44:5)

Historically, Israel was a nation that came from the lineage of Jacob. From a national perspective, Israel was a collective of people born out of the bondage of Egypt. In this way, "*Israel*" was a physical family of people. Most importantly, however, "*Israel*" was also to become a symbol of the overall healing journey of humanity. Accordingly, just as the human being is both a physical entity and a spiritual being, so too is this Divinely-appointed nation. *Israel* is associated with the covenant of the Creator to a particular people, and is also representative of His ultimate purpose to raise humanity to our true, Spiritually-centered design. Thus, from the intention of Yah, Israel is both a physical nation and a Spiritual concept *at the very same time*. Neither of these realities negates the other.

As we are about to see, these realities are exquisitely woven together to bear the fruit of harmonious global healing.

The Hebrew Meaning

The meaning of the name "*Israel*" has deep implications for us. In Hebrew, it is "*Y'Isra'el*," and we can properly interpret the meaning by considering its origin in the book of Genesis. We will find its first Biblical appearance in Genesis chapter 32 where we visit the amazing night of Jacob's wrestling with a mysterious "*man*." It is valuable in our consideration of Jacob's life to remember that, while the Scriptures may very well be describing true historical events, particular life highlights have been chosen in this ancient communication to provide representative symbolism. This, I have come to understand, is really for the sake of our discovery of Divine, transcendent truths. What is the most valuable for us, therefore, is to discern what these people and events actually *do* represent.

Jacob Becomes Israel
Genesis 32: 24-32

"Then Jacob was left alone; and a man wrestled with him until the breaking of day.

Now when he saw that he did not prevail against him, he touched the socket of his hip; and the socket of Jacob's hip was out of joint as he wrestled with him.

And he said, 'Let me go, for the day breaks.' But he said, 'I will not let you go unless you bless me!'

So he said to him, 'What is your name?' He said, 'Jacob.'

And he said, 'Your name shall no longer be called Jacob, but Israel; for you have struggled with God and with men, and have prevailed.'

Then Jacob asked, saying, 'Tell me your name, I pray.' And he said, 'Why is it that you ask about my name?' And he blessed him there.

> *So Jacob called the name of the place Penuel: 'For I have seen God face to face, and my life is preserved.'*
>
> *Just as he crossed over Penuel the sun rose on him, and he limped on his hip.*
>
> *Therefore to this day the children of Israel do not eat the muscle that shrank, which is on the hip socket, because he touched the socket of Jacob's hip in the muscle that shrank."*

As we mentioned, the above narrative is the first time we find the name *Israel* appearing in the Hebrew Bible. When we review the details of this passage, we begin to discover important and startling keys to understanding what "*Israel*" can truly mean to hearts that are searching, and open to higher things.

Even though Jacob continues his life in a somewhat blinded manner for many years following that significant night, it is fascinating how the Scriptures symbolically portray this event as being an opening moment of *enlightenment*. Twice, we see the indication that Jacob's wrestling is taking place at night: directly before the *breaking of day*. The day was just about to dawn, and light was just around the corner. We can further see the concept of enlightenment being pictured, when, towards the end of this chapter, the narrative speaks of the *sun rising* upon Jacob as he is re-embarking on his journey.

Furthermore, it is noteworthy that the Hebrew word for "*breaking*" (of day) is "`*alah*," which means "*to ascend*" or "*to go up*." The concept of the day arising, combined with Jacob's declaration that he saw *God face to face* that night, speaks to us of an exalted connection with the Divine Consciousness. All of these details are included in the narrative to signal to the reader what it means to become enlightened. With this perspective in mind, we see that enlightenment is a key factor in what it means to become the *Israel* of the Creator's heart.

Even though Jacob does not live according to a completely enlightened consciousness after these events, *we* are blessed with the gorgeous opportunity to step into these principles of enlightened transformation, in *our* lives, through the amazing insights found in this particular Biblical narrative. The fact that Jacob is recorded to have evidently continued in his own personal struggle beyond this point of clarity, gives testament to the fact that every insight we gain will need to be tested against the gravitational pull of outside forces. We see in this, the Divine opportunity to build spiritual muscles by putting into practice what we have learned, ultimately so that we can master the art of rising above the current of base, collective consciousness.

Moving on in our consideration, the particular passage we're discussing opens with the following words:

> *"Jacob was left **alone**; and a man **wrestled** with him…"*

So what is our mind being directed to with this reference to *solitude* and *wrestling*?

When people begin a quiet mindfulness practice in their life, whether it takes the form of meditation, journaling, solitary time in nature, deep introspection, or something else: the common experience for people is that they are suddenly overwhelmed with a multitude of stressful, painful, or fearful thoughts. Why would this happen, when we're just trying to get quiet? The reason is simply because past pains, hurts, and stresses have remained stifled and concealed within the person. These painful feelings go unnoticed to the conscious mind, mostly because they are suppressed by the individual's incessant addiction to distraction, which can take many forms. Hence, whenever we stop the continuous stream of outward noise from diverting us away from our inner experience, then buried thoughts and feelings begin to rise to the surface. For some people, this feels so painful that they quickly decide against meditating, or they avoid being alone (without an addiction at hand), at all costs.

Beginning the introspective process of *meeting yourself*, and concurrently allowing past traumas and fears to come to the surface in order to face them: this parallels Jacob's spiritual *wrestling* in the narrative. When we are quietly alone with ourselves, we have the opportunity to become *aware* of the struggle that we *already* have going on inside ourselves.

The underlying experience of this personal conflict will continue as long as we fearfully resist the flow associated with true spiritual connection. Once we genuinely connect with the exalted Consciousness that is above all noisy, egoic thoughts: we find authentic freedom, and the wrestling finally comes to an end. Through our trusting allowance, we step into the dimension of transcendence, and we rise above the conflictive nature of fear.

There's an obvious question that arises when we ponder these things. Specifically, just what is it that we are programmed to fight against? What are we in resistance *to*, exactly? On the surface, we may be resisting what we don't like in our lives. We may resist behaviours in others that upset us. We may resist painful circumstances. Yet, underneath all of this surface resistance, usually lies a bedrock of inner turmoil. When we continually resist what is happening in our lives, we keep ourselves resistant to seeing the hand of the Divine at work, and we numb ourselves from the lessons that are intrinsically present. Much of our difficulties are of our own creation, and the painful consequences must be acknowledged and accepted for what they are, if we are to learn and grow from them.

Even if we didn't directly create a challenge in our lives, within the difficulty, there is Divinely intended opportunity for meaningfully growing into our true selves.

One particular sense wherein people frequently practice inner resistance is in the way that our outward self, suppresses our true, inward self. This is because our inward self is always seeking to be expressed, yet we resist our true, unique expression because of fear. Curiously, we have been programmed to be afraid of expressing who we actually are at our core.

Fear of failure, fear of being rejected, fear of responsibility, fear of loneliness, fear of not being good enough, fear of embarrassment... all of these fears keep us small, and they prevent our true self from being manifested.

Nevertheless, when we begin to look at these things from a higher place, we realize that there is no need to be fearful of any of these things. We realize that we are still doing perfectly fine: if we fail, if we are rejected, if we have obligations, if we are lonely, if we aren't 'good enough,' or if we are embarrassed. In fact, peacefully allowing these elements in our life-walk is a very important part of being humble and vulnerable in our quest for true growth. When we are centered within ourselves, we grow when we fail; we grow when we're embarrassed; we grow when we realize we're not 'good enough' in-and-of ourselves. By facing our fears, and no longer giving them opportunity to continue to block our path, we realize that the very things we feared are actually - intrinsically - part of the beautiful path to health and wholeness. It is stunningly fitting that the *way to the Tree of Life,* in Eden, was guarded by a cherubim with a flaming sword. As we move closer to the Divine Presence in the midst of the garden, we find that our fears have to face the fire, and afterwards dissolve away from our person.

It's important for us to admit that when we resist our higher calling, we also resist the hand of the Divine in our life. The insanity of this is that, by so doing, we unconsciously stand against our own victory: none of us can stand against the Divine and actually *win*. Moreover, such a stance on our part is absurd when we realize that our Creator is fundamentally rooting *for* us – for who we truly are. He is *against* the very things that are destroying humanity, but He is *for* everything that is good, healing and supporting. We simply need to embrace the reality that we will experience apprehension at times in our journey of development, and learn to move in the direction of growth, anyway. This is an inherent part of truly loving ourselves.

When we see that Jacob is *alone* and *wrestling* at the beginning of the narrative, it is reminiscent of the chronic inner conflict that the spirit of humanity has commonly learned to accept, and even cling to. Early in childhood, virtually all of us developed the programmed tendency to inflexibly resist whatever we didn't like in our lives. To most people, this actually seems like the only way to survive unpleasant circumstances and situations. Yet, there is a much better way that we are being called to, according to our true design. And, most importantly, it's the only way to genuinely find success. In short, we need to become someone who has tapped into the ability to completely *soar above* the apparent problems that show up in our pathway.

Soaring above these things will mean that we have learned to dwell in trust. It means that we live in peaceful, trusting acceptance of *what is*, while believing that painful experiences will melt away as we move forward in our authentic growth. It also means that we begin to view problems in a different light. We discover within difficulties the opportunity for learning, growth and transformation. We start to see problems as a learning experience, for us to grow into a new and better person.

> *"For whom YHWH loves He reproves, even as a father the son whom in whom he delights. How blessed is the man who finds wisdom and the man who gains understanding."* (Pro. 3:12)

By the end of this momentous night in Jacob's life, after connecting with the Divine Consciousness, he is prophetically given the opportunity to realize the *true self* and to become one who prevails – being renamed *Israel*. It is so true that genuine healing does not come when we persist in wrestling, resisting, and kicking-and-screaming throughout the course of our lives. Alternatively, we will find healing by dwelling in love and trust, and thereupon prevail, as we discover *our* inward Israel.

When Jacob was left to himself, no longer distracted by the noise of the outer world, he was able to enter inside himself, and face his fears. He was finally able to observe *Who it Is* that he has been fighting with, throughout his life. The Divine Consciousness appears to him, and demands to be "*let go*." Yet, can we *actually* hold the Divine captive? Not really. But we can certainly hold the true-self captive, which was originally designed to align with the Divine Consciousness, having been made according to the glorious *likeness* of the Creator. This inner part of us is always seeking to be made free, yet we can unconsciously keep ourselves in chains. We have been conditioned to cover-over our hearts with layers of stone, no longer free to be the open space for the *Source River of the Spirit* to flow through.

That night Jacob was given insight into what it means to be truly blessed. Though he had been relentlessly pursuing blessing in his life by means of being a *heel-catcher* from his birth, he was finally discovering that genuine blessings come by freeing the captive heart, and becoming open to the Divine.[8] On this occasion, Jacob's determination is graphically portrayed when he expresses that '*I will not let this man go, unless I am blessed.*' This is a unique moment in Jacob's life, where he is finally seeking to be blessed by a Divine Source, rather than through the outward Esau that he had been clinging to throughout his life. In this moment, his desire for Divine blessing was fulfilled through the promise of a new name, and all that it signified. He was instructed that true blessing would come by no longer being called *Jacob*, but *Israel* instead.

The record in Genesis chapter 32 reveals that the real context for becoming Israel is that "*you have **struggled** with God and* *with men, and have prevailed."* In this phrase from verse 28, the common English translation of the word *"struggled"* is a bit misleading, however. In Hebrew, the word for *"struggled"* is *"sarah"* which actually means *"to have power, or successfully prevail as a leader or commander."* The word *sarah* thus signifies a primary definition of *"Israel."* Israel is the one who has successfully *prevailed* – with God – and with men.

When we look at all of the information provided to us, we are given a very powerful definition of Israel: *The Prevailing Prince with El.*

This is what it means to authentically *be* Israel. It means that we look to the true Source of blessing, which has always been the Spirit of the Divine. It means that we unlock the flow of the Divine into our lives, by opening the door within ourselves. It means that we trade hearts of stone for hearts of flesh. It means that we see God *face to face.* It means that we stop wrestling, and stop resisting the movement of the Creator in our lives. It means that we become who we were born to be, by rising above the finite realm of outward physicality so that we may finally *prevail.*

"Moreover, I will give you a new heart and put a new spirit within you; and I will remove the heart of stone from your flesh and give you a heart of flesh." (Ezekiel 36:26)

We find even more valuable gems when we delve a little deeper into the narrative. This is particularly true, when we discover the insights contained in the following statement:

*"So Jacob called the name of the place Penuel: 'For I have seen God face to face, and **my life is preserved**.'"*

First of all, it is fascinating how this declaration of Jacob stands in contrast to the Nimrod-styled systems of men. Nimrod was one who had stood in God's face, figuratively blocking the Creator from the view of those who were looking to him for deliverance. Yet, in this case, Jacob's experience of the Divine is such that he is able to see God 'face-to-face.' This narrative allows us to glimpse what it means to have authentic connection with the Spiritual realm, in contrast to the continual false perception that is the prerequisite to renouncing the true-self under the influence of rigid religious systems and / or social ideologies.

Secondly, the Hebrew word for "preserved" is "*natsal*" – meaning "*to snatch away*," or "*to deliver*," in the sense of snatching someone (or something) from the grip of another party. With this meaning in mind, it is interesting to consider what this implies to Jacob's circumstances. The question is, whose grip was Jacob being freed *from*? Jacob had been deathly afraid of Esau's anger towards him, yet it was Jacob who was the *heel-catcher*. He was the one clinging to Esau the whole time, and he needed to let go. And, while he needed to let go of the heel of Esau, even more significantly, he needed to loosen his grip on *himself*, and let the *true self* within go free.

When our true self becomes awakened in our present consciousness, we no longer have to chase anything outside of ourselves. We no longer seek after the Nimrods of the world in our efforts to *feel* connected. When we open ourselves up, and free the authentic self within us, we are freed from the grip of the external consciousness that we had previously identified with. We insightfully realize that we are much more than we had previously been aware.

The narrative closes with Jacob leaving Penuel, limping upon his leg. It is fascinating to consider the relevant Hebrew that describes his physical condition. It is said that a tendon or ligament in his thigh had "shrunken." The Hebrew word for *shrank* is "*nasheh*" – meaning "*to fail,*" coming from a root word that means "*to forget.*" In this, it would seem that we are being cued into the perception that the path of Jacob was still to be affected by an inward disconnection following this encounter with the Divine.

Based on the Biblically recorded future events that were yet to unfold, we know that Jacob did not come away from this night of wrestling having been immediately transformed. He had many years of healing ahead of him, as he struggled to rise above the unhealthy mentality that he had developed in his earlier years. He had to face many difficulties along the way, including the uncomfortable consequences of his failures to properly lead his family.

"…few and evil have been the years of my life…" (Gen. 47:9)

Yet, despite Jacob's ancient failures, it is still phenomenal to consider that these recorded events are highly instructive for us, thousands of years later. We too are called to become "*no more Jacob:*" to no longer be those who cling to the external, false, egoic, collective consciousness. We are all being developed, to emerge as Israel: to become one who is elevated in royal alignment with the Divine King of the Universe, and who has splendidly matured into the majestic, and glorious, *Prince With El*.

The Journey of Jacob

In order to fully glean the representative symbolism found in Genesis, it will be helpful to briefly review the earlier narrative of Jacob's life.

Following is Jacob's early life in summary:

- Jacob was a grandson of Abraham, and the son of Isaac and Rebekah. Rebekah had been barren, but after Isaac had pleaded with God to allow her to conceive, she became pregnant with twins, who were even said to be struggling within her womb. In relation to this, she received the Divine communication that there were "two manners" of people within her. These twins were to be very different in appearance, in personality, and in character. Esau, which means "hairy" or "rough," was born *"red"* with hair covering his entire body *"like a hairy garment."* Jacob was born grasping the heel of Esau, and given the name that means *"heel-catcher."*

- Esau is described in the narrative as a *"skillful hunter"* and a *"man of the field."* Jacob, on the other hand, was called an *"upright man,"* who *"dwelt in tents."*

- The narrative goes on to tell us of how Esau sells his birthright to Jacob, for a mere pot of stew. We are also told of Isaac's effort to bless Esau, the son he loved, and of how Jacob tricks Isaac into believing that *he* is actually Esau, by dressing up in animal furs and pretending to be his hairy twin brother. Since Isaac was blind, Jacob is successful in deceiving his father, and he essentially steals the fatherly blessing away from Esau.

- In response, Esau becomes so angry that he seeks to kill his brother Jacob, and Jacob feels forced to flee from his family. Jacob then travels to meet his relatives in Haran. Upon arrival in Haran, he falls in love with his relative, Rachel, and in order to buy her hand he sells himself into slavery to Rachel's father, Laban. After the seven years of agreed upon servitude, Jacob is deceived and given Leah (Rachel's sister) as wife, and has to commit to another seven years for Rachel's hand.

- Eventually Jacob leaves Haran with his wives and children, to return to the land of Canaan. He had acquired many riches in Haran, after his years of servitude had ended, and Genesis chapter 32 finds him on the road back to the dwelling place of his fathers. Esau had apparently heard of his return, and travelled to meet Jacob on the way. This was a most distressing discovery to Jacob, as he had no idea what ill feelings may have been retained by his brother after all these years. Naturally, Jacob thought it very plausible that Esau was coming to attack his household.

These details form the background of what we find in the wrestling of Jacob, in Genesis chapter 32.

From Esau, to Jacob, to Israel.

We can certainly consider the events in Jacob's life from many angles, and thereby receive numerous lessons to inform our own transformational journey. At present, however, we will particularly consider the symbolism associated with the journey of Jacob's life: *from Esau, to Jacob, to Israel*. This is the journey of every true human being.

Esau: The egoic, false, external self.

To understand the events in Jacob's life journey, we also need to consider the role that Esau plays in Jacob's life. It is no coincidence that Jacob and Esau are twins. It is also no coincidence that Esau is born *first* and that he is covered with hair, like the fur of an animal. In this way, it is no stretch to consider that, from a symbolic perspective, Esau is synonymous with reactive, animalistic consciousness. This reactive, base consciousness can be equated to the egoic, false, external self.

Esau is also said to have been *red* upon his birth. The Hebrew word for *red* ("'*admoniy*," from "'*adam*") speaks to us of the physical formation of Adam from the dust. In this sense, Esau is synonymous with the *mere* physicality of the biological human, and is therefore symbolic of what it means to live according to a consciousness that is only attuned to the world of *physical form*. In essence, to identify with Esau is to live in the world of chemical-physicality, while being simultaneously cut off from our Spiritual potential – not to mention our connection to the Divine. This is the world that we are all *first-born* into. If we are to become more than this, then first, we will need to deliberately *choose* to commence on a personal journey towards our true potential.

Allegorically speaking, Esau was the non-identical *twin* of Jacob for the purpose of demonstrating that we all have a particular *twin* with which we identify early in life. This identification is chiefly because of the programming and social / familial acculturation of our early years. In no way, however, does this twin resemble our *true self*. Esau came out first (as the firstborn) to signify that, when we are born into the world, we are *immediately* faced with circumstances that constrain us to become an inauthentic version of ourselves, as we attempt to adapt to the distorted environment we find ourselves growing up in. In this case, Jacob's authentic expression of self was adversely influenced by the fact that his father "*loved Esau,*" because he ate of his venison. In some way, Isaac's egoic addiction skewed his ability to receive his *true* son; in view of that, Jacob did not feel free to be himself in his youth.

Jacob: The self on a journey.

Jacob is the physicality of our personhood, which is first born into an egoic world. This is the adopted circumstance wherein we will immediately begin facing conditioning that will teach us to identify with the external, egoic consciousness. The physical self thus begins life in this world, clinging to the heel of the egoic, false *Esau*.

In the life of Jacob we see that he seeks a birthright, and the blessing of his father, *through* this false ego. As we mentioned, the record specifies that his father "*loved*" Esau. In other words, Isaac (who fittingly becomes a blind man), loved Jacob's *false* self, in symbol. In particular, we are even told that Jacob goes to the extent of literally covering himself with animal fur, in order to trick his father into blessing him. Yet, was Jacob really blessed in this? Not likely in the way Jacob anticipated, since the words of Isaac did not directly manifest into Jacob's life. Instead, immediately following this 'blessing' he was forced to flee from an enraged brother, and he enters into years of servitude.

Jacob first tried to find blessing through that which belongs to Esau. He *bargains* for Esau's birthright, and *deceives* for Esau's blessing. Yet Jacob is a man who was said to *dwell in tents*. He is a nomad on a journey of development, and enlightenment. In this way, the real, magnificent promise for Jacob is that he will one day reach his potential, and finally be blessed to *become* Israel.

We are specifically told that God "loved Jacob" and "hated Esau," in the Scriptural record (Mal. 1:2-3). What does this mean in the context of a loving, just and patient God? Well, since Jacob is a representative element of the journeying-self, on the road to discovering who we were designed to be: it is therefore stated that he is loved of the Divine. The truth is, the Creator deeply loves us, even in our stumbling – whenever we are on a journey towards better things. Esau, however, is the element of the *false self*. God loves our true essence, but we can never have a relationship with the Divine by means of our external ego. We may curiously find acceptance from our earthly parents by becoming someone other than who we truly are, but this is not so with the Creator of the Universe. He is calling us to discover who we really are and, concurrently, to enter back into that love relationship with Him.

Israel: The inward, Spiritually-connected, true self.

To become what *Israel* represents, is the ultimate purpose of the journey of Spiritual transformation. It is the Heavenly calling for all of humanity. Like Jacob, every Spiritual seeker is on a journey to awaken to this Presence within. By original design, our inward-self aligns with the Divine; it is, therefore, through the process of going inward that we will be marvelously blessed to find the joyous riches of infinitely expressing our real essence. And, though it may seem *easy* to simply "go inward," the challenge will arise when we have to face the layers of subconscious pains, fears, beliefs and ideologies that stand in the way of our progress. We will need to develop the innate ability to rise above all of these things – in order that they may dissolve, and become something we no longer cling to in our person. In this way, we will open ourselves up to the limitless flow of Divine Consciousness, and connect with that which is eternal.

In Genesis chapter 25 (v.23), it is promised that two manners of peoples would originate from *Jacob and Esau*; as they would each become a national collective through their offspring. While this was to be fulfilled in a literal sense, it is also true that it was to be realized symbolically, as well.

Esau-esque people are those who are driven by reactive reasoning, and are detached from the higher self. This is the generalized human collective in our day, and has been for millennia. Rather than spiritually progressing, those driven by Esau characteristics tend to be rigid, stagnant, and keep themselves identified with the outward ego. The danger of the Esau-collective is that they are prone to behaviours that are unconscious, careless, discriminatory, and highly-

reactive in their dealings with one another. This is the
source of so much unnecessary conflict, and it is the reason
the world has known immense violence and war throughout
its history.

The contrasting *Jacob-esque* collective of people are those who
are no longer stationary, having embarked on a journey of
transcendent awakening. They have moved beyond fear-
based immobilization, and are beginning to discover that
they are more than what they have been programmed to
believe. This "*Jacobic*" journey is the process of going deeper
into the profundity of the true self, and into the very midst
of the Creator's Presence. The gorgeous paradox of this
reality is that the very same road that travels into the depths
of our soul, also rises to increasingly greater heights as we
learn to connect to the Consciousness of the Divine.

> *"For YHWH is the great God, and the great King above all gods.
> In His hand are the deep places of the earth; the peaks of the
> mountains are His also."* (Psa. 95:3-4)

> *"And it will come about in the latter days that the mountain of the
> house of YHWH will be established as the chief of the mountains.
> It will be raised above the hills, and the peoples will stream to it."*
> (Mic. 4:1)

The Twelve Scepters

The symbolic journey of Jacob is further developed in the
Scriptures with the offspring of Jacob literally growing into
the nation of *Israel*. From Jacob was born twelve *sons*, and
accordingly, we see Israel emerging as a nation comprised of

twelve *tribes*. There is great Spiritual significance in this national formation, and the essence of what this nation represents is of amazing value to us. By understanding the ultimate purpose of the Creator with Biblical Israel, we tap into the true core of our own humanity.

It is first beneficial to note that, in the wilderness, the Divine order of the encampment was such that these twelve tribes were divided into four groups, all of which were to be situated encircling the structure of the tabernacle. In other words, the tribes were to be encamped with the Presence of the Creator directly in their midst. Yet again, we see that the true spirit of *Israel* is synonymous with a population of people who have each tapped into their deep inner identity, and thereby have become authentically aligned with the infinite dwelling place of the Divine. The encampment of Israel also speaks to the fact that, whenever more than one of us is deeply connected to God, He becomes exponentially involved in our interactions with one another. We can begin to see Him in all of our relationships and there arises an incredible sense of vibrant aliveness in the collective midst.

When we begin to consider the Hebrew meaning associated with the word "*tribe*," we also uncover an amazing gem that compounds on the truths we have already been discussing. In fact, we find that to translate the original Hebrew into "*tribes*," gives no justice to the real meaning. After studying the Hebrew, it becomes stunningly clear that the true essence of what is being gorgeously relayed to us, is that the twelve divisions of this nation are expressly "*The Twelve Scepters*." How remarkable this is for us, in light of all that we have studied thus far.

There are two distinct Hebrew words that we see most frequently translated as *tribe* in the context of Israel, and they both appear to carry a similar meaning. These Hebrew words are as follows:

1. One Hebrew word commonly translated as "*tribe*" is "*shebet*"

2. The other word commonly translated as "*tribe*" is "*matteh*"

The following table provides a comparison of these two Hebrew words:

1 – "Shebet"	2 – "Matteh"
From an unused Hebrew **root word** with the probable meaning of "*to branch off.*"	From the Hebrew **root word** "*natah,*" meaning "*to stretch out, extend, spread out.*"
Both of the Hebrew words, *Shebet* and *Matteh*, which we commonly see translated as "*tribe*," convey a similar meaning of: "***a rod, staff, scepter, or branch.***"	
The concept of tribal *branches*, in one sense, is figurative of the tribes of Israel having branched off from their forefather, Jacob.	
It is also decidedly significant that these two Hebrew words are often used of rods, staffs, and scepters, in the context of leadership and authority, and "*Matteh*" is the particular word that refers to the rod, or staff, of Moses.	
Appears 190 times in the Hebrew Bible	Appears 251 times in the Hebrew Bible

Meaningful Verses Where "Shebet" Appears:	Meaningful Verses Where "Matteh" Appears:
Gen. 49:10 "The **scepter** shall not depart from Judah, nor a lawgiver from between his feet, until Shiloh comes; and to him shall be the obedience of the people."	**Exo. 4:2,17,20** "So YHWH said to him (Moses), 'What is that in your hand?' He said, 'A **rod**.'..." "And you shall take this **rod** in your hand, with which you shall do the signs..." "Then Moses took his wife and his sons and set them on a donkey, and he returned to the land of Egypt. And Moses took the **rod** of God in his hand."
Gen. 49:28 "All these are the twelve **tribes** of Israel, and this is what their father spoke to them. And he blessed them; he blessed each one according to his own blessing."	
Num. 24:17 "I see Him, but not now; I behold Him, but not near; a star shall come out of Jacob; a **scepter** shall rise out of Israel, and batter the brow of Moab, and destroy all the sons of tumult."	**Num. 1:4** "And with you there shall be a man from every **tribe**, each one the head of his father's house." **Num. 36:9** "Thus no inheritance shall change hands from one **tribe** to another, but every **tribe** of the children of Israel shall keep its own inheritance."
Psa. 2:9 "You shall break them with a **rod** of iron; you shall dash them to pieces like a potter's vessel."	**Psa. 110:2** "YHWH shall send the **rod** of Your strength out of Zion. Rule in the midst of Your enemies!"
Psa. 23:4 "Yea, though I walk through the valley of the shadow of death, I will fear no evil; for You are with me; Your **rod** and Your staff, they comfort me."	**Isa. 9:4** "For You have broken the yoke of his burden and the **staff** of his shoulder, the rod (*Shebet*) of his oppressor..."

Psa. 45:6 "Your throne, O God, is forever and ever; A **scepter** of righteousness is the **scepter** of Your kingdom."	**Mic. 6:9** "YHWH's voice cries to the city—Wisdom shall see Your name: Hear the **rod**! Who has appointed it?"
Isa. 14:5 * "YHWH has broken the staff of the wicked, the **scepter** of the rulers." *(* Both Hebrew words appear in this verse)*	**Isa. 14:5** * "YHWH has broken the **staff** of the wicked, the scepter of the rulers." *(* Both Hebrew words appear in this verse)*

The twelve tribes are twelve facets of leadership and authority. The *Prince With El* collective of people *together* hold the staff of comprehensive leadership. Ultimately, they become the people who have finally manifested what it means to express the *image* and *likeness* of Divinity, carrying the responsibility of *dominion*, as Servant-Guardians in the earth.

In one manner, the Biblical nation of Israel is indeed a physical nation, which descended from Abraham, Isaac and Jacob. The beautiful uniqueness of the heritage of this literal nation, is that they have become a witness to all people, specifically in manifesting the journey that we are all being called to. In the history of Israel, we see the pitfalls of humanity being clearly exposed and, even more than this, we also see our own glorious calling, and the promise of healing, enlightenment and exaltation.

In another manner, *Israel* is a representative, all-encompassing truth for all of us. Like the physical, ancient nation of Israel, we too are called to leave the various Egypts of our past, and enter into a close bond with the Creator. We are called to connect with the Magnificent Divine *in our midst*. We are called to glorious victory over the false strongholds that lie in our path to abundance. We are called to peacefully trust, and no longer to fear. We are all called to enter into the gift of our heritage, and become part of the vibrant, shining, Divinely-appointed *royal family*.

> *"But the path of the just is like the light of dawn,*
> *that shines brighter and brighter until the*
> *fullness of day."* (Pro. 4:8)

Not one of us has been called to exercise authoritarian control over others; this has never been the purpose of the Creator for any human being. Individually and collectively, we are being called to a symphonic harmony of unique leadership roles: perfectly fitted to our varying talents and abilities.

The multiplicity of *twelve scepters* speaks to us of balanced diversity within this genuine *Israel* collective of people. Each individual is to fulfill their distinctive function of leadership in the context of the wider, holistic, healthy community. Regardless of what pursuit we feel moved to focus on, we will be blessed to learn from one another's wisdom and expertise; we will align with certain mentors along the way; and we will sit at the feet of various teachers. Accordingly, at other times, *we* will be the mentor, the teacher, the expert, the leader – providing a source of inspiration and education to others in their walk. As long as we continue to progress, and grow in wisdom, skill, trust, humility and love, we will become an ever more precious gift to the rest of humanity.

The symbolism of the *twelve scepters* illustrates to us the concept of being part of the Creator's family, and being part of His Kingship. These scepters of authority speak to a harmonious collective of humanity, ruling in perfect unity and oneness *with* Him. He has invited us to *lead with Him*. What a gorgeous and unspeakable gift. It seems almost too good to be true, yet it is the truest thing in the world. It is His purpose – His glory – His joy – to have His family gratefully joining with Him, in loving care for all life in His creation.

The true picture of what God has been planning from the beginning is thoroughly woven throughout the fabric of His perfect design. It is the ultimate message intertwined within the books of the ancient Hebrew Scriptures. In this we see that the Creator's expressed purpose for humanity has never changed. We have lost sight of it, we have lost track of it, but He has not. He will still lovingly fulfill in us what He had always planned from the beginning. He still plans to show to us our true essence. He still plans to reveal to us the beautiful *wholeness* that we were created to be from the very beginning.

Essentially, each of us will personally need to learn to become a *scepter-holder*, which is gorgeously representative of our deep, intimate connection to the Divine Creator. In symbol, it *is* the trust that we place upon Him and the confident state we decidedly learn to dwell *within*. When complete, holistic trust overwhelms our spirit, we are then made whole, and fitted to become the skillful leader of our calling. Ultimately, we hold this glorious scepter: by holding His hand, by dwelling in His love, and by respecting the universal laws that govern the creation.

When we find ourselves rightfully holding this scepter, we will have been transformed into that which is signified by *Israel*. Finally, when the entire planet becomes filled with *scepter-holders*, Divine glory will fill the whole earth. It is then that we will all know the Infinite One to Whom no definition can reach. It is then that His Kingdom of ultimate love will be all that there is.

> *"And no longer shall each one teach his neighbor and each his brother, saying, 'Know YHWH,' for they shall all know me, from the least of them to the greatest, declares YHWH."*
> (Jer. 31:34)

> *"… all the earth shall be filled with the glory of YHWH.'"*
> (Num. 14:21)

In the truest sense, we are all Israel. We always have been. For generations, we have been led into believing that our identity is tied with our first-born twin Esau; we have heard only the false, external, painful song of the world around us. Yet, our true self has always been there, from the beginning, waiting for us to awaken to ourselves.

The Divine Creator has invited us to walk with Him, on the majestic road that winds ever-upward and searches ever deeper – as we move towards *who we really are*.

This day can be our day, to connect with *Our Leadership Calling*, and to *Rise Above the Illusion of Fear*.

NOTES

1. See Exo. 33:11:
   "So YHWH spoke to Moses face to face, as a man speaks to his friend."

   [Note from Chapter 1, page 4]

2. See 1 Sam. 8 – The people of Israel demand a King:

   "Now it came to pass when Samuel was old that he made his sons judges over Israel. The name of his firstborn was Joel, and the name of his second, Abijah; they were judges in Beersheba. But his sons did not walk in his ways; they turned aside after dishonest gain, took bribes, and perverted justice.

   Then all the elders of Israel gathered together and came to Samuel at Ramah, and said to him, 'Look, you are old, and your sons do not walk in your ways. Now make us a king to judge us like all the nations.'

But the thing displeased Samuel when they said, 'Give us a king to judge us.' So Samuel prayed to YHWH. And YHWH said to Samuel, 'Heed the voice of the people in all that they say to you; for they have not rejected you, but they have rejected Me, that I should not reign over them. According to all the works which they have done since the day that I brought them up out of Egypt, even to this day — with which they have forsaken Me and served other gods — so they are doing to you also. Now therefore, heed their voice. However, you shall solemnly forewarn them, and show them the behavior of the king who will reign over them.'

So Samuel told all the words of YHWH to the people who asked him for a king. And he said, 'This will be the behavior of the king who will reign over you: He will take your sons and appoint them for his own chariots and to be his horsemen, and some will run before his chariots. He will appoint captains over his thousands and captains over his fifties, will set some to plow his ground and reap his harvest, and some to make his weapons of war and equipment for his chariots. He will take your daughters to be perfumers, cooks, and bakers. And he will take the best of your fields, your vineyards, and your olive groves, and give them to his servants. He will take a tenth of your grain and your vintage, and give it to his officers and servants. And he will take your male servants, your female servants, your finest young men, and your donkeys, and put them to his work. He will take a tenth of your sheep. And you will be his servants. And you will cry out in that day because of your king whom you have chosen for yourselves, and YHWH will not hear you in that day.'

Nevertheless the people refused to obey the voice of Samuel; and they said, 'No, but we will have a king over us, that we also may be like all the nations, and that our king may judge us and go out before us and fight our battles.'

And Samuel heard all the words of the people, and he repeated them in the hearing of YHWH. So YHWH said to Samuel, 'Heed their voice, and make them a king.' And Samuel said to the men of Israel, 'Every man go to his city.'" (NKJV)

[Note from Chapter 1, page 9]

3. For clarification: when looking at the Hebrew meaning of "*serpent*," which is Hebrew "*nachash*:" it is based on its Hebrew root word, "*nakhash*" wherein we find that the meaning is "*to hiss or whisper.*"

[Note from Chapter 4, page 38]

4. Studies that consider the neuroanatomy of the brainstem and cerebellum, and /or note anatomical similarities with reptiles:

- Myers, B., Scheimann, J. R., Franco-Villanueva, A., & Herman, J. P. (2017). Ascending mechanisms of stress integration: Implications for brainstem regulation of neuroendocrine and

> behavioral stress responses. *Neuroscience And Biobehavioral Reviews, 74*(Part B), 366-375.
> - Reiter S, Liaw H, Yamawaki T, Naumann R, Laurent G. On the value of reptilian brains to map the evolution of the hippocampal formation. *Brain, Behavior And Evolution [serial online]*. 2017;90(1):41-52.
> - Fuchs, E., & Flügge, G. (2003). Chronic social stress: effects on limbic brain structures. *Physiology & Behavior, 79*(3), 417-427.

[Note from Chapter 4, page 50]

5. Apart from bringing a clean animal to offer, the bringing of the firstfruits of harvest are typically regarded as an acceptable offering (among many), according to the Torah. Also, it is important to note that it is the best of the beginning of our produce, for any given time-frame, that we are to bring – wherein we will be blessed. (see Lev. 23:10-14; Deu. 26:2-4; Pro. 3:9; Eze. 44:30; Neh. 10:35).

[Note from Chapter 5, page 57]

6. For reference, following are a few Social Science studies demonstrating the importance of healthy community:

> - Boothroyd, R. I., Flint, A. Y., Lapiz, A. M., Lyons, S., Jarboe, K. L., & Aldridge, W. A. (2017). Active involved community partnerships: Co-creating implementation infrastructure for getting to and sustaining social impact. Translational Behavioral Medicine, 7(3), 467-477.

- Van Harmelen, A., Kievit, R. A., Ioannidis, K., Neufeld, S., Jones, P. B., Bullmore, E., & ... Goodyer, I. (2017). Adolescent friendships predict later resilient functioning across psychosocial domains in a healthy community cohort. Psychological Medicine, 47(13), 2312-2322.

- Freedman, D. A. (2017). Promoting healthy communities for population health. In M. A. Bond, I. Serrano-García, C. B. Keys, M. Shinn, M. A. Bond, I. Serrano-García, ... M. Shinn (Eds.), APA handbook of community psychology: Methods for community research and action for diverse groups and issues (pp. 361-375). Washington, DC, US: American Psychological Association.

[Note from Chapter 5, page 68]

7. "El" in Hebrew means a singular "Mighty."

[Note from Chapter 6, page 91]

8. In Hebrew, the name "Jacob" literally means "heel-catcher." He was given this name to reference the manner of his birth, in which he was born grasping the heel of his firstborn twin brother, Esau.

[Note from Chapter 7, page 114]

About the Author

Yiskah Rose embraces a deep
interest in open-minded, Biblical
Spirituality. She has been studying
the Scriptural message for over two
decades: with a current focus on the
ancient Hebrew Scriptures.

With a voracious spirit of curiosity, her research is
carried out while asking the prayerful questions of
*"God, what do You want us to know, and what do You want
us to see?"* In this, she joyfully continues to seek deeper
connection with the ultimate truth that has emanated
from the heights of the Divine Consciousness.

Yiskah is also a wife, and a homeschooling mother of
three beautiful boys. She enjoys spending her days
being present with her family, and practically pursuing
wellness and growth in all areas of life.

www.ingramcontent.com/pod-product-compliance
Lightning Source LLC
Chambersburg PA
CBHW051651040426
42446CB00009B/1091